ADVANCE PRAISE FOR
COMMON FINANCIAL SENSE

Harris Nydick and Greg Makowski have provided the building blocks to plan and execute successfully for your retirement. Long before Common Financial Sense *was written, Greg taught me that making small, informed changes immediately made big and positive differences in my situation. This guide delivers the most practical and straightforward tutorial I have ever read.*

HAZEL O'LEARY
FORMER UNITED STATES SECRETARY OF ENERGY

Harris and Greg have many years' experience helping employees with their 401(k) accounts and have used that experience to write this very readable book. I wish I had access to this book earlier in my career! I promise to pay it forward by sending a copy of Common Financial Sense *to each of my three 20-something kids.*

SKIP SCHWEISS
PRESIDENT, TD AMERITRADE TRUST COMPANY

Common Financial Sense *is a breath of fresh air and should be required reading for everyone entering or in the workforce. Nydick and Makowski slice through the jargon and deliver a clear explanation of how to understand the value of the 401(k) plan so you can retire successfully. Their many years of teaching others have resulted in a brief, to-the-point book that delivers a valuable lesson that will last a lifetime.*

DEAN DURLING
PRESIDENT AND CEO, QUICKCHEK CORPORATION

Common Financial Sense *by Harris Nydick and Greg Makowski is a must-read for any individual who has aspirations of living comfortably in retirement during their "golden years." The sheer brilliance of this book is its simplicity, which should be well received by any investor who seeks better control of his or her financial destiny. If you are interested in a better understanding of how markets can assist you in meeting your financial goals, turn off the "experts" on cable television and go purchase this book.*

MICHAEL PIETRONICO
CEO AND SENIOR PORTFOLIO MANAGER,
MILLER TABAK ASSET MANAGEMENT

Common Financial Sense *is a call to action that dispenses the kind of wisdom that we all need but don't know how to get. Harris Nydick and Greg Makowski have written an insightful new guide that simplifies and demystifies retirement plan investing. Read this book! It will help you make smart decisions to successfully pursue your financial goals.*

JOSHUA PACE
PRESIDENT AND CEO, TCA BY E*TRADE

Harris Nydick and Greg Makowski have provided those striving for financial security in retirement with a real gem in Common Financial Sense. *Critical and complicated concepts regarding stocks, bonds, credit, savings, expenditures, and other financial concepts are presented in a way that is understandable and enjoyable to read. Any retirement plan participant and those who wish they were would do well to sit down and read this book. It will change the way you think about and prepare for your financial future.*

RICHARD LYNCH, AIFA
DIRECTOR, FI360 GLOBAL FIDUCIARY INSIGHTS

Common Financial Sense *teaches financial literacy without requiring any previous investment, financial, or math skills. This book should be a core assignment in high schools, colleges, and universities everywhere. Harris and Greg provide many spot-on examples that will help you plan well. Don't try to go through the retirement maze alone; you'll only be one day closer to retirement without a real plan.*

DAVID E. MARCUS
CEO AND CHIEF INVESTMENT OFFICER,
EVERMORE GLOBAL ADVISORS, LLC

COMMON FINANCIAL SENSE

FOREWORD BY **TED BENNA**

THE INVENTOR OF THE 401(k) AND CO-AUTHOR OF *401(k)s FOR DUMMIES*

COMMON FINANCIAL SEN$E

Simple Strategies for Successful 401(k) & 403(b) Retirement Plan Investing

HARRIS NYDICK, CFP®, AIFA® **& GREG MAKOWSKI**, CFP®, AIF®

LIONCREST
PUBLISHING

*This book may be purchased in bulk for promotional, educational, or
business use. Please contact the authors by email at cfs@cfsias.com.*

COMMON FINANCIAL SENSE
Simple Strategies for Successful 401(k) &
403(b) Retirement Plan Investing

ISBN   978-1-5445-1029-3 *Paperback*
            978-1-5445-1030-9 *Ebook*

CONTENTS

A NOTE TO OUR READERS

The views and opinions expressed in this book are solely those of the authors. The information presented has been obtained from sources we believe to be reliable. As such, the authors are not responsible for any errors. None of the information provided is intended to be nor should be construed as tax, legal, or investment advice of any kind. All examples in this book are hypothetical, do not reflect actual investment results, and are not guarantees of future results. Investment returns, inflation, taxes, and other economic conditions may vary from the presented assumptions. Indices mentioned are unmanaged and cannot be invested into directly. There are risks involved with investing, including possible loss of principal and lack of liquidity. The investment return and principal value will fluctuate so that an investor's shares, when sold, may be worth more or less than their original cost. As such, the authors specifically disclaim any responsibility for liability or loss incurred by utilizing the concepts presented herein. Investors should consider the investment objectives, risks, charges, and expenses of the investment company carefully before investing. The prospectus contains this and other information about the investment company. Prospectuses may be obtained from your advisor and should be read in full. Please consult with your investment or financial planning professional before making any investment decisions.

ACKNOWLEDGMENTS

First and foremost, we consider ourselves to be students at all times. Therefore, one of our primary objectives is to learn something new every day. We are fortunate to live a life filled with gratitude. We love what we do, respect who we do it with, and appreciate who we do it for.

Thank you to all of our mentors, teachers, and clients. You are the reason we are able to help people reach their financial and retirement goals. Thank you to everyone at CFS Investment Advisory Services, L.L.C. We have the best team in the business, and you are the backbone of our professional support system. Thank you to all of our families and friends, the core of our personal support system.

We learn from you all. Today and every day.

HARRIS NYDICK AND GREG MAKOWSKI

FOREWORD

BY TED BENNA

Designing and implementing the first 401(k) savings plan during the fall of 1980 was the high point of my career as a benefits consultant. At least 50 million employees have utilized 401(k) since then to accumulate $15 trillion of retirement savings including amounts rolled from these plans into IRAs. Many participants have thanked me for designing a plan that has helped them successfully retire.

These plans convert spenders into savers. I know because, like most workers, I would have never accumulated on my own the amount I built up in my 401(k) account. The 401(k) isn't complex. It is merely a plan that helps employees save for retirement by making *saving* a priority. This is important because workers need an income to replace their paychecks when they retire.

Creating a plan that will help you successfully replace your income at retirement is where the complexity begins. This requires many decisions, including when to start, how much to contribute, how to invest, how much will be needed, when to retire, and so on. These aren't easy decisions, but help is available.

A bit of history may be useful at this point. There is a widely held myth that we once had a wonderful retirement system where everyone received an employer-funded lifetime pension when they retired. Many politicians state this as fact during campaign season. For starters, defined benefit pension plans never covered more than 30 percent of the private sector workforce. This is the type of plan that provides a monthly check for life.

My first employer was Provident Mutual Life Insurance Company. Provident Mutual had a pension plan. Male employees weren't eligible until age 30 and female employees weren't eligible until age 35. You also had to stay at Provident Mutual until age 60 to get any benefits. These were typical provisions in those days. Some employers were noted for getting rid of long-term employees when they were close to fulfilling the vesting requirements. Business failures during that era resulted in a lot of additional suffering because many retirees and active employees lost all or a substantial portion of their pensions.

Congress eventually passed the Employee Retirement Income Security Act (ERISA) in 1974. This bill strengthened the private pension system in the short run; however, a couple of its provisions are major factors resulting in the death of the private pension system. I know, because I sold and administered pension plans before the passage of ERISA. ERISA included a provision putting a portion of corporate assets of companies that had a pension plan at risk. Accountants warned their clients not to adopt one of these plans, making it impossible to sell them.

ERISA also imposed maximum limits on pension benefits for the first time. That provision broke the financial linkage between rank and file employees and senior executives. Post ERISA, senior executives could no longer benefit from increasing pension benefits, so they looked elsewhere. Today, non-qualified retirement plans limited to senior executives and stock option plans are the big wealth-generators for top management rather than the pension and 401(k) plans that cover all employees.

The accounting profession also played a role in the demise of pension plans by changing the accounting standards in a way that made pension expenses unpredictable. As a result, senior executives were and are still able to improve the potential of a big payoff via stock options by replacing a pension plan with an enhanced defined contribution plan.

You may be wondering at this point why I include this information about the decline in traditional pensions at the beginning of a 401(k) book. The first reason is that it gives me an opportunity to debunk the myth that we once had a wonderful private retirement system that 401(k) killed. The second reason is to stress the fact that 401(k) was never intended to be the backbone of the private retirement system. It was a political fluke that I helped to turn into something much bigger than was ever intended. You can check the history on my website: www.benna401k. com. The last reason is also to help you understand the political risk to our private retirement system.

ERISA was enacted to help preserve the private defined benefit pension system. It did that in the short term, but it is a major reason why pension plans will continue to decline. It is having the opposite long-term impact than was intended. The provision that added Section 401(k) to the Internal Revenue Code was only one-and-one-half pages long. It wasn't expected to be a big deal. I helped change that by interpreting this section of the code in a very different way than what was intended. So, you never know what the long-term impact will be when Congress changes the tax laws. The result can be very different than what was intended.

Tax reform is currently in the news again. The last major tax reform effort was during Ronald Reagan's presidency.

The first version of his Tax Reform Act would have killed 401(k) plans. That effort failed due to a very strong lobbying effort; however, the maximum annual contribution limit was reduced from $30,000 to $7,500. Without question, 401(k) plans will receive attention as tax reform moves forward. One idea usually floating around is to totally remove the pre-tax advantage forcing employees to save after-tax.

Now that all this is out of the way, I will attempt to set the stage for the information that follows. Like it or not, the burden of planning for retirement is yours—no one else is going to do it for you. Successfully planning for retirement in today's environment isn't easy. Careful planning is needed and the earlier you start, the better. If you are looking for a book with a lot of fluff, this isn't it. If you are looking for a book that contains a magical solution, this isn't it. This book does, however, contain a wealth of solid, basic information from Harris's and Greg's many years of hands-on work with 401(k) participants. Following their suggestions will enable you to substantially improve your odds of retiring successfully.

One last thing. One of the most frequently asked questions is whether I tried to patent my 401(k)-savings-plan design. The answer is yes, but I was told it wasn't possible. If I had been successful, perhaps I would have benefitted financially from each participant. The fact that I haven't is okay.

However, there is a way you can show your appreciation if you feel inclined to do so by donating to Compassion International. Through them, you can sponsor a child in need or contribute to one of four special projects: Water and Sanitation, Health and Nutrition, Youth Development, and Survival. Go to www.compassion.com for more information. They are a great organization.

TED BENNA

OPENING THOUGHTS: WHY IS COMMON FINANCIAL SENSE SO UNCOMMON?

"Everyone thinks of changing the world, but no one thinks of changing himself."

LEO TOLSTOY

This book is for people who are ready to take responsibility for their financial future but need some assistance in understanding how to approach their 401(k) plan. While we will reference the term *401(k)*, everything covered in this book also pertains to 403(b) retirement plans. Feel free to use the terms *401(k)* and *403(b)* interchangeably, because the plans are set up and run in a very similar fashion. The main difference is that 401(k) plans are retirement plans for companies and 403(b) retirement plans are for nonprofit organizations, including schools, museums, churches, and charitable institutions.

In high school, there should have been a course called "Practical Finance." This class would have provided a real-life approach to financial matters that would benefit every graduate. Topics would have included how to write a check properly, how to balance a checkbook, understanding how credit cards work, what a credit rating is, and how to establish and maintain that good rating. The course also would have explained how 401(k) retirement plans work, because these are skills that everyone will need to master. To our knowledge, this class is still not taught at our former high schools, although some states have gotten the memo. Since Vermont's Champlain College issued its first state-by-state report card for personal finance course requirements in 2013, there have been some improvements. Still, only five states earn the A grade with a full semester of personal finance required, while 11 states have absolutely no requirements for personal finance and are marked with a failing F grade.[1]

This confusion plays out now in corporate America on a regular basis. At some point, after you have been hired, you receive an email that tells you that you are now eligible to

---

1   Champlain College, 2017 National Report Card on State Efforts to Improve Financial Literacy in High Schools, https://www.champlain.edu/centers-of-excellence/center-for-financial-literacy/report-national-high-school-financial-literacy.

join the company's 401(k) retirement plan and that you need to sign up with a deadline coming soon. You see all kinds of terms that look unfamiliar to you. You are most likely given an email address or 1-800 number for any questions you may have. Any questions you may have? Somebody in the HR department sure has a cruel sense of humor.

You have so many questions you don't even know where to start. You may have participated in a previous employer's plan, but those decisions were somewhat random, and you certainly don't want to do anything randomly this time. Once again, you feel like a deer in the headlights, and you think to yourself that there must be a better way to approach this important aspect of your financial life.

This book hopes to provide the information about 401(k) plans that we all wish we knew when we were starting our careers. No matter what stage of life you are in, the information we are about to present will be helpful to you. No special knowledge about investing or retirement plans is necessary, as everything will be presented in plain English with as little lingo or jargon as possible. That is what we call common financial sense.

It is not our purpose to get into a history lesson about the demise of the guaranteed pension plan in America, nor is it meant to take any specific political point of view. There are other volumes that delve into those matters.

The intent of this book is to give you practical ideas that make common financial sense and will help you navigate your retirement planning journey successfully. We each have over 30 years of experience successfully helping hundreds of companies, and many thousands of their employees understand one of the most important financial investments you will make over your lifetime: the 401(k) retirement plan.

First, what is a 401(k) plan? A 401(k) plan is a retirement plan that is available through your employer. Named after the section of the Internal Revenue Code in which it appears, a 401(k) plan is an arrangement under which you can elect to have a portion of your compensation contributed and invested as a reduction in salary.[2]

We understand that you probably spend more time planning your summer vacation than you do planning your financial future. We get it. The facts actually back you up. A 2015 Employee Benefit Research Institute study reveals that people really do spend more time planning social events and planning for the holidays than they spend on planning for retirement.[3] Join us as we guide you through

---

2   Employee Benefit Research Institute, History of 401(k) Plans: An Update, February 2005. https://www.ebri.org/pdf/publications/facts/0205fact.a.pdf.

3   Employee Benefit Research Institute, 2015 Retirement Confidence Survey. Ruth Helman, Craig Copeland, and Jack VanDerhei, "The 2015 Retirement Confidence Survey: Having a Retirement Savings Plan a Key Factor in Americans' Retirement Confidence," EBRI Issue Brief, no. 413 (Employee Benefit Research Institute, April 2015), page 13. https://www.ebri.org/pdf/briefspdf/EBRI_IB_413_Apr15_RCS-2015.pdf.

this brief book; it has been written to help you make better-informed decisions about how to plan for your financial needs and wants during your retirement years.

This book is divided into two sections. Section One (Chapters One through Five) briefly discusses the major external issues that need to be considered in your planning for retirement. Section Two (Chapters Six through Fifteen) covers the major issues directly involved with your 401(k) planning.

Over the years, we have heard many stories from employees at enrollment and education meetings that simply aren't true. We put these stories in the category of retirement myths. We address some of the most common retirement myths in shaded sections within the corresponding chapter throughout the book.

Recognize up front that almost everything we discuss in this book is logical. There's one problem, however. For most people, money is not a logical issue—it's an emotional one. We have asked many clients, "Could you handle a sudden drop in the market and your account of 15 percent even if you knew it would eventually come back?" Virtually all say "yes." As a follow-up question to clarify the issue, we ask, "So you're okay with a $15,000 loss with every $100,000 you have invested?" and the response is always, "I never said that!"

It's not easy to reconcile the logical issues of money with the emotional ones. You can look at it as if there are two trains: the emotional train and the logical train. The only time these two trains are on the same track is when they're heading right toward each other!

As mentioned earlier, common financial sense as a concept is the ability to understand and reconcile logic and emotion, enable us to prevent making decisions that we'll later regret, and achieve financial independence upon retirement. We may not realize it, but when we start our careers in the working world, we own the gift of time. Assuming that you begin working in your early 20s and work until your mid-60s, you can expect to work for approximately 45 years. That 45-year period is the gift of time we will talk about. While you may change jobs, some things don't end up as you originally planned. If fortunate enough to remain in good health, 45 years down the road, we're all going to arrive at the same spot on the map of our lives—retirement.

Hand-in-hand with the gift of time is the gift of compounding returns. Put simply, compounding returns are cumulative over time, adding more and more to the original amount. Investopedia describes it this way:

"The wonder of compounding transforms your money into a state-of-the-art, highly powerful income-generating tool. Compounding is the process of generating earnings on an asset's reinvested earnings. To work, it requires two things: the reinvestment of earnings and time. The more time you give your investments, the more you are able to accelerate the income potential of your original investment, which takes the pressure off of you."[4]

This may be why Albert Einstein is credited with saying that "compound interest is the eighth wonder of the world. He who understands it earns it...he who doesn't...pays it."[5]

This may be the only 45-year investment goal that you can count on reaching. The single biggest mistake we see made is not recognizing this fact. If more of us understood it for what it is, then with one 45-year time horizon, it would make sense to build one 45-year investment plan. How often is that done? Almost never, because there are so many distractions that occupy our lives in this regard. At the first sign of the market going down abruptly, let's change the plan. At the first sign of market strength, let's change the plan. You can see how quickly this vicious cycle devolves our one 45-year plan into a series of three 15-year plans, nine 5-year plans, and, ultimately, forty-five 1-year plans. It happens without even recognizing the

---

4   Investopedia, "Investing 101: The Concept of Compounding." http://www.investopedia.com/ university/beginner/beginner2.asp?ad=dirN&qo=investopediaSiteSearch&qsrc=0&o=40186.

5   Calaprice, Alice. *The New Quotable Einstein*. Princeton, NJ: Princeton University Press, 2005 (pp. 294–295).

behavior, because we are too busy reacting to short-term facts that will most likely have little or no bearing on our long-term outcome.

What if you don't have the gift of time? What if you're not 25 anymore but are now 55? Actually, you still have the gift of time, but you may not realize it. As you read on in the next chapter, chances are very good that you'll live longer than you think you will.

Does that mean that you should remain fully invested at 65? Probably not, but you're not going to turn into a pumpkin at the stroke of midnight on your 65th birthday either. So don't invest too conservatively. When asked what their biggest financial regrets were, our senior clients responded in many ways, but the two things near the top of everyone's list were that they wished they had saved more money and they wished whatever they did save was invested more into stocks and less into bonds and savings accounts.

INVEST WITH GOALS

⊘ What does your idea of retirement look like?

⊘ Where do you want to live?

⊘ What hobbies and activities would you like to participate in?

⊘ How do you plan on financing it?

⊘ Create long-term financial goals and start working toward them.

SECTION ONE

CHAPTER ONE

LONGEVITY

"Life is a journey, not a destination."

RALPH WALDO EMERSON

Twenty-five years ago, while on vacation in southern Florida, our family walked into a Walmart store for the very first time. On that day, we needed to pick up suntan lotion, an important item that we had forgotten to bring. Living our entire lives in the suburbs of northern New Jersey, we never experienced Walmart before because it had not yet set up shop in the tri-state area.

What is the first thing you encounter whenever you walk into a Walmart? The greeter. The greeter is obviously there to greet you in a friendly manner. The greeter is there to help direct you to the aisles and to assist you in navigating the store easier. The greeter is almost always over the age of 65.

This greeter, an elderly gentleman, was friendly and gracious. He sent us right to where we needed to go and minimized our confusion in this otherwise alien setting. We were in and out of the store quickly, and my wife said to me, "That was amazing!" Walmart is brilliant for having an older person greet you at the door, because it feels like you are being welcomed home. She continued, "All that was missing was the smell of fresh cookies baking."

From a marketing perspective, she was correct in concluding that Walmart had successfully delivered that message. However, I had a completely different takeaway from our brief encounter with the greeter. "Are you kidding me?" I asked. "That was frightening! There's an older gentleman who has already worked a lifetime, long enough that he could and should be retired already."

We know that there's a percentage of folks who work past age 65 because they want to, though most who work past that age do so only because they must. If the greeter had planned his finances better, maybe he wouldn't have to be working at that age. Sure enough, the United States Department of Labor Bureau of Labor Statistics reports that the percentage of people between the ages of 65 and 69 who are working grew from 21.9 percent in 1994 to 32.2 percent in 2016.[6]

---

6   United States Department of Labor, Bureau of Labor Statistics, Civilian Labor Force Participation Rate, by Age, Sex, Race, and Ethnicity, Table 3.3. https://www.bls.gov/emp/ep_table_303.htm. Last updated on October 24, 2017.

Instead of blaming "the system," it is important for us to take responsibility for the decisions we make, especially our financial decisions. Making better financial decisions leads to better financial outcomes—outcomes that should reduce the need for over 32 percent of the people aged 65 to 69 in the U.S. to work past their normal retirement age.

How long are we going to live? The answer may surprise you, and you may be really shocked to learn that in all probability, it will be longer than you think. Let's take a look at Figure 1-1.

LIFE EXPECTANCY PROBABILITIES
If You're 65 Today, the Probability of Living to a Specific Age or Beyond

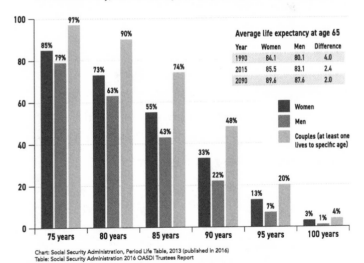

Chart: Social Security Administration, Period Life Table, 2013 (published in 2016)
Table: Social Security Administration 2016 OASDI Trustees Report

Figure 1-1. Life Expectancy Probabilities (Source: J.P. Morgan Asset Management Retirement Insights, *Guide to Retirement*, 2017. Used with permission.)

Figure 1.1 demonstrates that one in five men and one in three women who make it to 65 will go on to live to 90 years of age. If you are a couple, the odds of one of you living a very long life increases substantially. At age 65, the chances that one of the two of you will live until age 80 is 90 percent, and there's still a one-in-five chance that one of you will live at least until age 95.

Average life expectancy continues to increase each year due to medical advances and more people taking better care of their health through better lifestyle choices—including smoking less, eating properly, and exercising regularly. The average life expectancy at age 65 for men in 1990 was 80.1 years and 84.1 years for women. By 2015, it had increased to 83.1 years for men and 85.5 years for women.

By 2090, it is projected that the average 65-year-old man could expect to live more than 87.5 years, and a 65-year-old woman could live more than 89.5 years.[7] That's a lot of birthday candles. More importantly, it means you'll need a lot of money to fund all those years of retirement. You likely need to plan for a retirement that could last 30 years or more.

---

7   J.P. Morgan Asset Management Retirement Insights, Guide to Retirement, 2017 Edition, Life Expectancy Probabilities, https://am.jpmorgan.com/us/en/asset-management/gim/adv/insights/guide-to-retirement, page 5, February 16, 2017.

Someone very dear to us once said that any problem solved with money isn't a problem. What he meant was that without your health, any amount of money wouldn't be of much use to you for very long. Take good care of yourself, so you can enjoy your retirement and make the financial sacrifice worthwhile.

INVEST FOR THE JOURNEY

⊘ **There are no do-overs.**

⊘ **Plan to live a long life, perhaps longer than you think.**

⊘ **Remain physically and emotionally healthy so you can enjoy more active years.**

⊘ **Life is a journey, not a destination. Prepare financially for each stop along the way.**

CHAPTER TWO

SOCIAL SECURITY

"Life's tragedy is that we get old too soon and wise too late."

BENJAMIN FRANKLIN

The Social Security Act was signed into law in 1935 by President Franklin D. Roosevelt. One of the Act's major provisions was a formula to provide a lifetime retirement income for retired workers beginning at age 65. To fund the Act, taxes started to be collected in 1937 and payments began in 1940.

Age 65 was not an arbitrary choice. At the time, the average 21-year-old man starting his work life could expect to retire at age 65 and then expect to collect Social Security retirement benefits for almost 13 years after that.[8] In 1983,

---

8 Social Security Administration, Social Security History: Life Expectancy for Social Security. https://www.ssa.gov/history/lifeexpect.html.

the full retirement age was increased on a sliding scale up to age 67 for workers born in or after 1960.

As it was originally designed, Social Security retirement income benefits still provide an important portion of the money needed to fund the expenses you will incur in your retirement years. The plan is very flexible, and as such, there are many ways to collect Social Security retirement income benefits. You should visit www.ssa.gov to monitor your payments into the system and to track the amount of anticipated benefits the government may provide.

Reduced lifetime benefits may be collected beginning at age 62. As of this writing, full retirement is for those workers reaching age 66 this year. You can also delay filing to collect benefits until age 70. If you file to collect at age 62, the monthly benefit amount is permanently reduced by 25 percent to 30 percent of your full retirement amount. If you wait until age 70, your monthly income amount will be permanently increased, currently by 32 percent (up to 8 percent per year from age 66 to 70).[9] Of course, you won't collect any benefits during the four years between age 66 and 70.

The breakeven point for any of these decisions is between 12 and 15 years, so you need to decide what is best for your

---

9   Social Security Administration, Social Security Benefits: Early or Late Retirement? https://www.ssa.gov/oact/quickcalc/early_late.html.

personal situation. Sometimes your situation determines your decision. According to a 2017 EBRI Retirement Confidence Survey, even though 75 percent of pre-retirees expected to work until age 65 or longer, only 23 percent were able to do so. Of those who left the workplace earlier than planned, 41 percent retired because of health problems or disability. Another 26 percent retired early either because of downsizing at their company or because the company closed down entirely, and 14 percent left to care for a spouse or another family member.[10]

RETIREMENT MYTH #1

"When I retire, I can live off of my Social Security check." We hear this sometimes too. According to the Social Security Administration, Social Security retirement benefits are structured to replace approximately 40 percent of your pre-retirement income.[11] The average amount a person currently receives in Social Security benefits totals approximately $16,000 a year. Very few people can live on only 40 percent of their pre-retirement income. Even if you could, is that really what you would prefer to do instead of setting aside some money now for the future?

---

10   Employee Benefit Research Institute, Lisa Greenwald, Craig Copeland, and Jack VanDerhei, "The 2017 Retirement Confidence Survey: Many Workers Lack Retirement Confidence and Feel Stressed About Retirement Preparations," EBRI Issue Brief, no. 431 (Employee Benefit Research Institute, March 21, 2017), page 20. https://www.ebri.org/pdf/surveys/rcs/2017/IB.431.Mar17.RCS17.21Mar17.pdf.

11   Social Security Administration, Understanding the Benefits, 2016. https://www.ssa.gov/pubs/EN-05-10024.pdf, page 1.

One of the most common questions we get about retirement and financial planning revolves around the possibility of Social Security going broke. We are asked, "Should I include the projected Social Security benefit amount in my retirement income planning?" Here is what we know right now based on current laws. According to the Social Security Board of Trustees, based on the theoretical combined trust fund reserves and current assumptions, full benefits should be payable to at least 2034, and approximately 75 percent of full benefits should be payable afterward.[12]

Congress will eventually need to increase the solvency of the Social Security retirement program. Changes that could be considered include increasing the full retirement age beyond age 67 for younger workers, increasing payroll taxes, and increasing or eliminating the wage cap on payroll taxes. The idea of phasing out Social Security benefits for recipients that have larger incomes from other sources is being discussed as another option.

Retirement income is not a Democratic or Republican issue; it is an American one. That's why we believe that the program will remain fully, or almost fully, intact for

12 Social Security Administration Blog, Carolyn Colvin, Acting Commissioner of Social Security, Social Security Funded Until 2034, and About Three-Quarters Funded for the Long Term; Many Options to Address the Long-Term Shortfall, June 22, 2016. http://blog.ssa.gov/social-security-funded-until-2034-and-about-three-quarters-funded-for-the-long-term-many-options-to-address-the-long-term-shortfall/.

the foreseeable future. Therefore, our answer is yes, you should include the projected Social Security benefit amount in your retirement planning.

Perhaps the more relevant question is, "Will I be here for Social Security?" You will pay a lot of money through payroll taxes into the Social Security system over your working life. While we have made it clear that the average person will live a very long time, make sure that you take steps to remain healthy so you can live long enough to get at least your fair share. Social Security retirement benefits are well-earned. They are important benefits, but the amount provided is not going to produce enough income to fully support you in retirement. It was never meant to.

INVEST FOR FINANCIAL STABILITY

⊘ There should be some sort of Social Security retirement benefit available to you, no matter what your current age is.

⊘ You must plan on supplementing your expected Social Security retirement benefit in order to have enough money to be able to retire.

⊘ Create financial stability for yourself by using Social Security as a base, then add other sources of retirement income from your 401(k) retirement plan and other savings and investments.

CHAPTER THREE

HEALTHCARE COSTS IN RETIREMENT

"It is health that is real wealth and not pieces of gold and silver."

MAHATMA GANDHI

Not many people think about the cost of healthcare (hospitals and doctors) and long-term care (assisted living and nursing home facilities) in retirement. It's an unpleasant topic, though it must be included in any discussion about financial planning for your retirement years. Additionally, basic things that we take for granted in our younger years—such as vision, hearing, and dental care—start to become expensive to manage as we age.

Medicare, Medicare supplemental insurance, and long-term care insurance cover some but not all of the expenses associated with these issues. A male retiring today can expect to spend, on average, approximately $245,000 on healthcare during his retirement, excluding nursing home and long-term care expenses.[13] Because of longer life expectancies, women may have to spend even more after retirement just to cover general medical expenses. If it's needed, long-term care costs now average more than $45,000 per year in an assisted living facility; a bed in a semi-private room in a nursing home carries an average charge of more than $85,000 a year.[14]

To get a handle on the shift in healthcare expenses that retirees can expect, we can look to the 2016 HealthView Insights data report on healthcare insights.[15] For a couple retiring today at age 65, Medicare premiums average $644 a month. By age 75, these premiums will escalate to $1,239 a month, and by age 85, $2,387 per month.

When you add up the costs for your Medicare Parts B, D, and Supplemental Insurance premiums over a 20-year retirement, it can add up to over $435,000. If you add in all of your out-of-pocket expenses, another $5,000-$10,000 a year is needed.

13   Fidelity Investments, Health Care Costs for Couples in Retirement Rise to an Estimated $245,000, https://www.fidelity.com/about-fidelity/employer-services/health-care-costs-for-couples-retirement-rise, October 7, 2015.

14   Genworth Financial, Inc., The Genworth Cost of Care Study, August 2017. https://www.genworth.com/about-us/industry-expertise/cost-of-care.html.

15   Health View Services, Health View Insights: 2016 HVS Retirement Health Care Costs Data Report, 2016., http://www.cfsias.com/blog/2016-hvs-retirement-health-care-costs-data-report.

If this weren't costly enough, in the Affordable Care and Modernization of Medicare Act, Parts B and D are now means-tested. In other words, as you make more money, you pay more in Medicare premiums.

Let's look at how this works. According to that same report, a 40-year-old earning $40,000 today can expect a 36 percent surcharge on his or her Medicare Part B and D premiums. So, if he or she is expecting to pay about $190,000 in premiums over his or her lifetime, the surcharge just added over $68,000 to his or her premiums. If he or she earns $75,000 today, then the surcharge will add an additional $380,000 in premiums—instead of planning on paying the $190,000, he or she will pay $570,000 in Medicare premiums. On top of this are out-of-pocket expenses, which can add another $100,000 in healthcare costs.

This doesn't take long-term care expenses into consideration either, because Medicare does not cover them. Depending on the state you live in, assisted living communities can average $573–$21,240 a month, and skilled nursing facilities can average $1,945–$42,948 a month. In-home care can average $1,525–$10,479 a month.[16]

---

16 Genworth Financial, Inc., The Genworth 2017 Cost of Care Study National and State Monthly Date Tables, September 2017. https://pro.genworth.com/riiproweb/productinfo/pdf/179702.pdf.

As you can see, healthcare expenses can quickly eat away at your retirement savings. The earlier you plan and save for these expenses, the greater the likelihood that you will be able to save enough money to sustain your normal standard of living.

ACKNOWLEDGE REALITY

⊘ Remember to plan for healthcare expenses as you prepare your retirement budget.

⊘ The reality is that your healthcare expenses are probably going to be much higher than you expect.

CHAPTER FOUR

INFLATION

"Inflation is taxation without legislation."

MILTON FRIEDMAN

Inflation is the ever-increasing cost of the things we buy and use. Think back to when you were a child. What did gasoline or mailing a letter cost? How much did you pay for your first car? When you look back in time, you realize that almost all of these goods and services were less expensive. Over time, the costs of all of these have gone up; that's inflation.

Let's get to some real numbers. In 1977, it cost $0.13 to mail a letter. By 1997, that amount rose to $0.32, and in 2018, it costs $0.50.

In 1996, a gallon of regular gas was $1.23, a dozen eggs were $1.11, a gallon of whole milk was $2.62, and a loaf of white bread was $0.88.

By 2016, these costs rose considerably, with $2.15 for a gallon of regular gas, $1.68 for a dozen eggs, $3.20 for a gallon of whole milk, and a $1.37 for a loaf of white bread.[17]

From 1996 to 2016, the average cost of these four items increased 44 percent. That's inflation.

Of course, these are national averages, and the actual prices vary by where you live. But in any region, you can see that the cost of everything has gone up over the past 20 years. What will the cost of food be 20 years from now? What will the price of a new home be? A new car? College? Healthcare? All these future expenditures are unknown, but you can be fairly certain they will all be more than you expect.

What this means to you is if you need $50,000 a year to live on now, then you may need $100,000 a year in 20 years and $200,000 a year in 40 years.

Social Security and a pension plan are forms of fixed incomes that will not keep up with inflation. If you have a fixed income, how do you make your money last through a retirement that hopefully continues for decades when the price of almost everything you buy increases every year? The only way to protect yourself is to invest right

---

17   United States Department of Labor, Bureau of Labor Statistics, All Urban Consumers (Current Series)/Top Picks, 2017. https://data.bls.gov/cgi-bin/surveymost?ap.

now in assets that have a history of growing faster than inflation. Stocks are one of the few assets that have a long-term history of being able to do this.

We also know that a dollar loses value against inflation because it costs more to buy the same basket of goods every year. That presents a tremendous opportunity for you, because you can take an asset that has less buying power over time (a dollar) and use it to buy an asset for your 401(k) retirement plan that has historically gained in value against inflation (a stock).

INVEST WITH PURPOSE

⊘ Inflation is a constant; prices go up just about every year.

⊘ Your big goals will need to be mostly self-financed.

⊘ Be ready for your future by beginning to invest for it now.

⊘ Be purposeful in choosing your investment strategy by making choices that keep pace with inflation.

CHAPTER FIVE

VERSUS

"*You always have two choices: your commitment versus your fear.*"

SAMMY DAVIS, JR.

You are going to need all of your emotional energy to succeed at retirement investing. The last few chapters dealt with most of the typical challenges you face in trying to plan for the future. However, the biggest obstacle you will encounter comes from within. The rest of our book offers a common financial sense approach to overcoming these and other issues. Before we move forward, let's take a look at some of the most confusing things about retirement investing.

Simple versus **easy**. This sounds like the same thing, doesn't it? We use them interchangeably in our language all the time. There can be a huge difference though. Let's look at the idea of weight loss. Losing weight is simple. If you eat less food (consume fewer calories) and exercise more (burn more calories), you will lose weight. Is it easy? Heck no. Weight loss is a multibillion-dollar industry. If losing weight is so simple, why isn't it easy to do?

Saving for retirement is similar. Spend less money and save more. That's all it takes. That's as simple as it gets, right? The idea of investing is simple too. Buy an investment and sell it for more. Is it easy? Of course not! In fact, it is one of the most challenging transactions we try to succeed at. First of all, acknowledge that this is a difficult task. Although anyone and everyone should be able to, many fail to achieve their financial goals by putting it off, going it alone, or taking advice from the wrong sources. The fact that you have avoided this topic until now is further proof that it's hard. If it were so easy, you would have already figured it out.

Scary versus **dangerous**. Spiders are scary. But only 30 of the more than 43,000 different types of spiders can harm a human.[18] Less than one-tenth of 1 percent of spiders are dangerous, but just about every type of spider scares most people. Almost all of them are completely harmless.

---

18 Britannica.com, Nine of the World's Deadliest Spiders, https://www.britannica.com/list/9-of-the-worlds-deadliest-spiders.

Investing can be very scary. One day your account is growing, and the next day it's falling. It's very difficult to make sense of it all. As we'll explain in the chapters ahead, it is rarely dangerous if you can manage to remain calm. Don't overreact to short-term situations; you must control your emotions.

Needs versus **wants**. Needs are basic things you must have to survive, such as a basic form of shelter, food, and water. Wants are things that you would like to have but could actually live without. For example, you need water to survive, but probably not the small bottle that sells for $3 at a store. The confusion between needs and wants happens whenever we make purchasing decisions of all kinds, especially technology (cell phones, computers, etc.), clothing, and cars. Although this is subject to your own interpretation, we have seen the blurring of needs and wants destroying too many financial plans for retirement. Take advantage of the free budget worksheet we offer in Chapter Seven. Complete it and follow the guidelines.

Do you really need to spend so much now at the expense of your future? Only you can determine the difference between your current financial needs versus your financial wants. You alone are responsible for setting aside some of your earnings from each paycheck for your future. It will arrive more quickly than you could ever imagine.

INVEST WITH WILLPOWER

⊘ In order to change, you've got to want to change.

⊘ Develop good saving and spending habits now.

⊘ Maintain your willpower as you embrace the life-long challenge of preparing for retirement.

SECTION TWO

CHAPTER SIX

HOW MUCH MONEY WILL I NEED TO RETIRE?

"Most people don't plan to fail. They fail to plan."

JOHN L. BECKLEY

Perhaps the most important question is, "So, how much money will I need to retire?" This simple question doesn't have an easy answer. There are quite a few ideas to contemplate. Popular wisdom says you will need between 75 percent and 85 percent of your current annual income to retire comfortably. However, we have found that there are no universal guideposts.

Everyone's idea of what his or her retirement lifestyle will cost differs dramatically. Some people prefer to have their mortgage paid off on their primary residence. Others want to leverage it to the hilt and take out a long-term mortgage upon retirement. They rationalize that their children and the bank can figure it out when they're gone. Others rent. You can see how quickly needs are dictated by the specific situations of those involved.

We do know that what started out as our life's to-do list morphs into our bucket list over time. This bucket list costs money, whether it's travel, hobbies, or other activities. Very little of what's on that list will be low-cost. Therefore, you can expect typical retirement financial needs to look like this: the first few years of retirement will cost more than 100 percent of your pre-retirement income.

After a few years of traveling and hobbies, people tend to settle into a routine that costs much less than their pre-retirement income. Then, during the last few years of life, expenses tend to skyrocket, as healthcare costs dramatically increase. There are many factors to consider, including assumed rates of return and asset allocation as well as your expected lifespan, to name a few.

The next consideration is how much money you can spend each year as a percentage of your total liquid investments. Many popular calculators assume that you can spend 4 percent of your principal each year, but of course, that requires regular monitoring as well.

Let's do some math using this formula. If you are married

and living on $80,000 a year while working, let's assume you'll need $64,000 (80 percent of $80,000) in retirement. As of January 2016, the average Social Security retirement benefit was $1,341 a month. If both of you are receiving your full Social Security benefits, this will provide approximately $32,000 a year of income.[19]

Therefore, you'll need to fund the difference of $32,000. An investment base of $800,000 at 4 percent payout will provide approximately $32,000 a year in additional income. These figures assume that Social Security will continue to pay their full benefits as promised (check your potential benefits by visiting the Social Security Administration's website at www.ssa.gov).

These figures do not include the effects of taxes or inflation. As we discussed in Chapter Four, inflation is difficult to predict, but we must assume that the cost of everything is going to increase over time. Since things are going to cost more in the future, your retirement income must increase at least as much as inflation or your quality of life will decrease over time. Taxes are another difficult assumption to predict because federal, state, and local income tax rates change over the years. You must make some assumptions and monitor them as things change from year to year.

---

19 Social Security Administration, Frequently Asked Questions, "What is the average monthly benefit for a retired worker?" https://faq.ssa.gov/link/portal/34011/34019/Article/3736/What-is-the-average-monthly-benefit-for-a-retired-worker.

If we take taxes and inflation into consideration, then the 4 percent payout you are getting on your portfolio must continue to grow over time to offset these ever-increasing costs. The only way for this payout to grow is to have part of your portfolio invested in stocks, because they are the only assets that have the ability to grow over time.

RETIREMENT MYTH #2

The most typical self-deception is that you believe that you have plenty of time until you retire, so there is no need to start saving now. It may give you comfort to say or even to believe it. The fact is that you need to set aside as much money as you can, as often as possible, in order to save enough for retirement.

Let's illustrate an obtainable and reasonable situation. An employee starts to contribute into his or her 401(k) plan account at age 25. At that time, he or she is earning a salary of $45,000 a year.

This person is going to contribute 6 percent of his or her income in his first year and will increase that amount by 1 percent a year until he or she hits the current maximum allowed by current law ($18,500 a year if age 49 or younger and $24,500 a year if age 50 or older). We're going to assume that he or she will receive salary increases of 3 percent a year and will earn 7 percent a year on his or her investments in the plan. Lastly, we assume that there is no employer match for this plan. Figure 6-1 shows the results.

RETIREMENT PLAN CONTRIBUTION ANALYSIS

End of Contribution Year	Salary Earned	Total Account Value			
		Starting at Age 25	Starting at Age 35	Starting at Age 45	Starting at Age 55
1	$45,000	$2,700	$2,700	$2,700	$2,700
5	$50,648	$21,687	$21,687	$21,687	$21,687
10	$58,715	$71,421	$71,421	$71,421	$71,421
15	$68,067	$166,098	$166,098	$166,098	
20	$78,908	$329,481	$330,708	$330,708	
25	$91,476	$568,502	$597,579		
30	$106,045	$928,247	$979,028		
35	$122,936	$1,456,833			
40	$142,516	$2,184,177			

Figure 6-1. Retirement Plan Contribution Analysis (Source: CFS Investment Advisory Services, L.L.C., 2018. Used with permission.)

Assumptions: Participant's starting salary is $45,000 in Year 1. Each year his or her salary increases by 3 percent. The participant starts with a contribution of 6 percent of salary and increases 1 percent each year until the current contribution, plus the catch-up limit, is reached. The investment portfolio has an assumed rate of return of 7 percent per year. All assumptions remain constant until participant's retirement at age 65.

At age 65, this person has a salary of $142,516 and an account balance of $2,184,177. As he or she contemplates retirement, the most important question is, "Can I afford to retire?" Assuming that he or she wants to continue spending approximately 80 percent of his or her pre-retirement income, they will require $114,013. Also, assume that he or she will remove 4 percent a year from his or her 401(k) plan account, which will provide over $87,000. Add in the amount of this person's annual Social Security retirement benefits, and he or she should have enough.

Not age 25 anymore? No worries at all. A 35-year-old pursuing the same strategy will retire with almost $980,000. If you're starting out at age 45, your balance will grow to over $330,000. Even someone beginning at age 55 will finish with more than $71,000.

No matter how much money you earn, these ratios and their relationships remain the same. You can achieve similar results. The only difference is that the younger you start, the more you'll have when you retire. Remember that this illustration assumes you don't save any other money from any other sources for your entire working life. Of course, it would be wonderful if you could save money in addition to your retirement plan. That additional savings should provide you with even more when you are ready to retire.

The purpose of this exercise is not to discourage you. It is intended to help us all have a clear recognition that we need to understand our 401(k) plan better and start investing as soon as possible. If you are already investing in your plan, increase the amount you are authorizing. It will take awareness and action on your part, but with motivation and discipline, it can be achieved. Continue reading on to the next chapter for some useful ways and ideas to save for retirement.

Retirement is the ultimate pass/fail course. Let's take a moment to review a very important logical and emotional concept, saving for retirement versus saving for your kid's college education costs. For most, emotion dictates that we set aside maximum funds so our child(ren) can attend the college of their choice. We're not advocating that you don't do this, but the logic here is very clear. There are scholarships for college; there are none for retirement. Perhaps you will qualify for financial aid for college, but there's certainly none for retirement. There are many types of student loans available for college. Loans for retirement? No such thing. The bottom line? You are going to need to pay attention to this.

STAY MOTIVATED

⊘ Start planning and saving right now.

⊘ The single largest determinant of how likely you are to reach your retirement goals is how much you invest in the first place.

⊘ It's not too late to start.

⊘ Stay motivated to succeed.

CHAPTER SEVEN

SAVE BETTER, LIVE BETTER

> *"It is not necessary to do extraordinary things to get extraordinary results."*

WARREN BUFFETT

We hear a lot of excuses why participants in 401(k) plans invest so little or not at all. Behind most excuses is a fear—a fear that the investments might lose money, a fear of the future, of not understanding how the plan works, of admitting that you don't understand it, and a fear that you don't have the discipline to live on a little less today so you can provide for the future.

There is a difference between an excuse and a reason. Behind most reasons is the unfortunate reality that no matter how much you currently earn, you truly can't cover your current expenses. Necessities like shelter, food, and clothing cost a lot of money. We understand that if you can't afford these essentials, then it's hard to think too far into the future. We totally empathize and respect your inability to contribute. All we ask is that you don't confuse a reason with an excuse. This chapter is intended to get you past some of the financial excuses you may have.

The ideal amount to be contributing to your 401(k) plan from your gross income is 15 percent. That is the amount many experts feel is necessary in order to accumulate enough money to retire.

Most people cannot afford to start out at that level. Assuming that you've got your basic expenses covered, start with a contribution amount of at least 1 percent of your pay. That's only $10 for every $1,000. If you can afford more, start with more. The most important step is to start. The next step is to increase that starting amount by 1 percent every year until you reach the 15 percent level. Even better, try to double the percentage every year—from 1 percent to 2, then 4, and so on.

Let's think about a few ways to find more dollars from your paycheck. If you haven't already done so, complete a personal budget and expense worksheet by going to the following link: https://goo.gl/j41yrL. Do this exercise in two ways. First, complete the budget worksheet on what you estimate your expenses to be. Then, use another copy of it based on your actual expenditures over the last 12 months. Compare the two, and you'll discover some discrepancies. Do either of the worksheets add up to the actual amount of income you bring in each year?

There's usually a difference, and for some, it is a large difference. Some of the money you'll need to find will turn up here. The rest will come from monitoring expenses that usually aren't included in your budget.

To rein in your budget, consider the 50/30/20 method of budgeting. This assumes that your fixed expenses comprise 50 percent of your spending. This includes housing, vehicle payments, and any recurring, usually necessary expenses. Then, 30 percent of your spending should be allocated to flexible spending, such as extra debt payments, entertainment, dining out, transportation expenses, and so on. The final 20 percent is divided for the future: 15 percent should go to your 401(k) retirement plan contribution and 5 percent to other investments and savings.[20]

There are a few easy ways to trim your budget to free up that final 20 percent so that you can fully contribute to your 401(k) plan. You can shop your cell phone plan and obtain a less expensive one. The same goes for your

---

20 Fidelity Investments, My Money 50/15/5 Guide, June 23, 2015. https://www.fidelity.com/mymoney/50155-guide-simple-approach-budgeting#Guide.

home entertainment bills—cable, Netflix, internet service providers, etc. There are many options now that can help you to save a bit here and there.

Use shopping and travel comparison apps. Drink your coffee at home or at the office and drive past the expensive coffee shops. Prepare your lunch at home and take it to the office instead of paying a higher cost of lunch at a deli. Don't indulge in the most expensive items on restaurant menus. Whenever you can, dine in a BYOB (Bring Your Own Bottle) restaurant and bring your own wine, beer, or mixed cocktails. Afterward, skip dessert and coffee in the restaurant and enjoy them at home afterward.

Make it even easier for yourself by playing the "Dollar a Week" game. In week one, try to save one dollar. Then, for each of the next 51 weeks, add an extra dollar to increase your savings by $1.00 each week. At the end of the first year, you will have saved $1,378. This is a fun way to jump-start your retirement savings.

While these small changes won't open up vast percentages in your budget, if you're vigilant about setting the money aside, they can make a difference. Remember that you only need to find $10 for every $1,000 to add another percentage to your investment. Together, they add up to savings that could easily make their way into your now-growing 401(k) account.

RETIREMENT MYTH #3

"I can't contribute because I don't make enough to put anything in." We hear that all the time. "Putting only $____ a pay period won't make a difference,'" is not true either. By definition, if you're not contributing to your 401(k) plan account, then you are saving nothing in one of the best tax-deferred ways available. Therefore, you're going to have nothing later on. Every dollar counts and adds up.

Let's take a closer look at the "Dollar a Week" game. If you invested the $1,378/year beginning at age 25, then you could have approximately $275,000 by the time you retire. Take a look at Figure 7-1. No matter how old you are when you start, that's a lot of money for someone who almost put nothing into his or her plan.

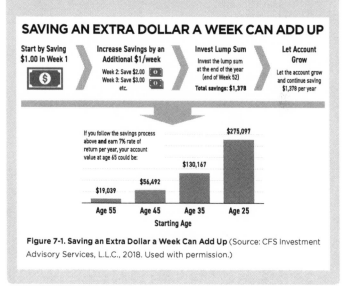

Figure 7-1. Saving an Extra Dollar a Week Can Add Up (Source: CFS Investment Advisory Services, L.L.C., 2018. Used with permission.)

We're not telling you how to spend your money. We are simply reminding you that your future will one day be here, and you don't want to be wondering *What if?* This is an instant gratification versus delayed gratification dilemma. You need to have the discipline to spend only some—not all—now so there will be more for tomorrow.

We understand FOMO (fear of missing out) and YOLO (you only live once). What are you spending your money on today that you should be setting aside for future FOMO and YOLO decisions? What will you tell your future self then?

INVEST WITH DISCIPLINE

⊘ Live your best life right now and plan for tomorrow's best life too.

⊘ Remember FOMO and YOLO, but don't forget HYPFTIR: How You Paying For That In Retirement?

⊘ A little saving adds up to a sizable amount over time.

⊘ Make a budget and live within it every month.

⊘ Stay disciplined and make it a way of life.

CHAPTER EIGHT

WHAT YOU CAN CONTROL VERSUS WHAT YOU CANNOT CONTROL

"Do not let what you cannot do interfere with what you can."

JOHN WOODEN

While there are many variables to consider when investing, it boils down to these five major issues: return, risk, time, emotion, and cost. As you'll see, these are all interconnected concepts. However, we focus almost all of our attention on the first one—return. What is the expected return on this investment? What has it done in the past? What return can we expect in the future?

We can't control return because we don't know if the investment markets will go up or down. However, we can control how much risk we take, how long we remain invested, our emotions, and the cost of the investment. Here's the irony: we rarely focus on the things we can control and completely focus on what we can't control. Why is that? Let's look at what we can control more closely and see if it might better inform our investment decision-making process.

We *can* control how much risk we take. Risk is a very interesting word because it means so many different things to many different people. As an example, if I asked 100 people to describe the word *orange*, almost everyone would describe it as a type of fruit or as a color.

Ask the same 100 people to describe risk as it pertains to investments and you will get many different answers. For some, risk means looking at your investment statement and seeing that it has gone down. For us, that's not risk; that's volatility. There's a big difference between investment volatility and investment risk, because the market goes up, down, and up again on a regular basis. It is a temporary state of being. To us, risk means that you arrive at age 85 in good health but have no more money to live on. Now what? Financially, it's game over. That's risk!

Perhaps that's the reason that we as investors don't like to focus on risk. If you take too much risk, you could lose your money and not have enough to live on in retirement.

If you take too little risk, you may end up running out of money because you never had enough to begin with. No wonder people avoid the subject! The optimal amount of risk is somewhere in between. We face these tradeoffs in our daily life but don't necessarily see it as such.

Have you ever spent the day at a large amusement park? When our children were younger, we used to take them to the Six Flags amusement park in the area. How many merry-go-round rides does it have? One. How many Ferris wheel rides does it have? One. How many roller coaster rides? Twelve. And each one is a measurement of how much risk you're willing to take that day.

Why is that? After all, the experience is virtually the same no matter which roller coaster you choose to ride on. You wait 45 minutes in a line, hop into the coaster, ride around for about a minute and a half while having your insides twisted, end up where you started, then go back in the line and do it again.

But something else is going on too. As you're walking around the park, you look at some of the coasters and think, "That one is no big deal." But you look at others, especially ones with names like the Pukemaster 2000, and what you think of them can vary from person to person or day to day. Some days, you might think, *There's no way I am ever going to ride that one*, so you choose one in between and hopefully enjoy the ride. Other times, you're in line for the one with the biggest dips and tightest turns.

The evaluation of which ride you're willing to go on is an evaluation of your perceived risk of losing your lunch that day. Might it change the next time you go to an amusement park? Maybe. That depends on other factors, such as how you're already feeling or how badly you want that hot dog.

Investing is similar. Before you choose an investment path, take a moment to define what an investment risk means to you. Understand and confront your fears, and you will already be on your way to overcoming them.

Don't forget that you can also control how much time you remain invested. Your time horizon for investment should be the amount of time that you expect to have before you need to use the money. We have already looked at time horizons of up to 45 years or more. Why would you run in circles created by 45 different 1-year game plans?

Time horizons are closely related to risk. The more time you have, the more risk you can take. Figure 8-1 shows the range of stock and bond annual total returns from 1950 to 2017, and it reveals some very interesting information.

Compare the annual returns of stocks, bonds, and a 50/50

blend of both over different periods of time. As you can see, the one-year returns are all over the place. Stocks have a one-year return of between 47 percent and -39 percent, and bonds are between 43 percent and -8 percent. The blend is between 33 percent and -15 percent.[21]

From this data, you are correct to conclude that investing over a short amount of time can be risky, sometimes with very bad results.

21 J.P. Morgan Asset Management Market Insights, Guide to the Markets, Range of Stock, Bond, and Blended Total Returns, Annual Total Returns, 1950–2017, January 2018, page 63. https://am.jpmorgan.com/us/en/asset-management/gim/adv/insights/guide-to-the-markets/viewer.

RANGE OF STOCK, BOND, AND BLENDED TOTAL RETURNS

ANNUAL TOTAL RETURNS, 1950–2017

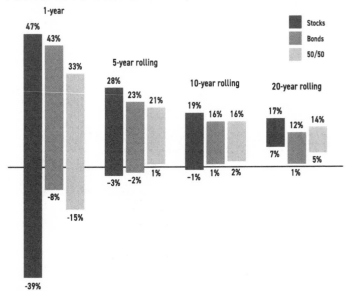

Figure 8-1. The Range of Stock, Bond, and Blended Total Returns: Annual Total Returns, 1950–2017 (Source: J.P. Morgan Asset Management Market Insights, *Guide to the Markets*, 2018. Used with permission.)

Assumptions: Returns shown are based on calendar year returns from 1950 to 2017. Stocks represent the S&P 500 Shiller Composite and Bonds represent Strategas/Ibbotson for periods from 1950 to 2010 and Barclays Aggregate thereafter.

Things shift dramatically when you look at the annual returns over rolling five-year periods of time. The ranges of returns tighten up, and the outcomes change, as well. The chances of a positive return are very high, and the range of negative returns is very small. This trend continues over 10- and 20-year rolling periods of time.

Over this same time frame, from 1950 to 2017, the average annual total return of stocks was 11.2 percent per year, and the annual average total return for bonds was 5.9 percent. A 50/50 blend of the two returned 9 percent per year.[22]

The longer your time frame, the longer you can remain invested. The longer you remain invested, the higher chance you will have a positive outcome. Historically, the chances of losses are strongly minimized over time, and the opportunities for gain are highly maximized due to the amount of time you remain invested, not due to the performance of any particular investment.

Emotion can be controlled, but there are times when our emotions get the better of us. This happens so often with investing precisely because money is an emotional subject, not a logical one. Let's take a look at what goes through your mind after you make an investment. After you have read, heard, or seen a story, you decide to invest.

At this point, you are optimistic. You have invested with the hope and expectation that the shares will rise and that you will profit from the decision. Then the value of your investment goes up a bit and excitement sets in. The shares continue to rise, and you are thrilled.

22 J.P. Morgan Asset Management Market Insights, Guide to the Markets, Range of Stock, Bond, and Blended Total Returns, Annual Total Returns, 1950–2017, January 2018, page 63. https://am.jpmorgan.com/us/en/asset-management/gim/adv/insights/guide-to-the-markets/viewer.

Furthermore, you begin to think, *Wow, I am smart!* The price continues up to a peak, and euphoria nearly overwhelms you. You don't recognize it at the time, but this is the point of maximum financial risk, because you and most everyone else think that the market can only go in one direction from here: up! You also don't realize that for the time being, the investment's price has peaked.

Now the investment's value starts to go down a bit, and you become anxious. It continues down a little more, and denial starts to set in. You think that this is a temporary setback. After all, you are a long-term investor. It slides further, and you become fearful. The price descends more, and now desperation is the emotion you feel, followed by panic as it sags some more. You reach the point of capitulation, where most people give up and sell out of their position at a huge loss.

You ask yourself, "How could I have been so wrong?" Despondency sets in, and sometime after that the investment reaches the point of maximum financial security, because its price lands at its rock bottom for this market cycle.

You may not even be paying close attention now, but the investment has started to rise slowly. Your mood has shifted from despondency to depression. You continue to monitor your stake as its price continues to go up and you become hopeful. It advances again as you begin to feel relieved, and you begin to think that this idea was good after all.

As the investment continues its upswing, you become optimistic about the market's prospects again.[23] You have now come full circle, and the entire emotional roller coaster starts again, as The Cycle of Market Emotions shows in Figure 8-2.

THE CYCLE OF MARKET EMOTIONS

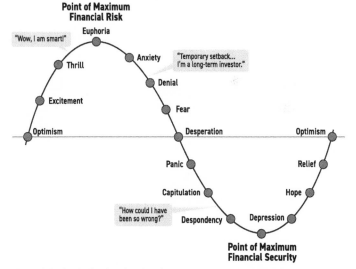

Figure 8-2. The Cycle of Market Emotions (Source: © Westcore Funds, Denver Investments, All Rights Reserved. Used with permission.)

---

23 Westcore Funds, Denver Investments, The Cycle of Market Emotions, All Rights Reserved, 1998.

Why is this important to understand? Because you are not the only one who feels this way as investments go through a complete market cycle. In fact, these are the typical emotions that virtually every investor experiences. It is human nature to have these feelings and experience these emotions as the value of investments rise and fall. Focus on what your initial investment was and how it has grown over time instead of being attached to what the investment's highest value once was. Many people concentrate on only the high point of each investment without admitting that virtually no one buys at the absolute low and then sells at its highest value.

It is vital to remember this exercise so that the next time you go through a market cycle, you stay the course. There's no way to know when the market has peaked or bottomed until well after it has occurred. You need the discipline to remain calm throughout the market cycle. It's easy to say but incredibly difficult to do.

Do not be overconfident when markets rise and do not overreact when markets fall. Maintain emotional balance. Remember that on the good days, you're not that smart—because on the bad days, you're not that misguided either.

It's because of these emotions that most investors earn a lot less than the returns of the financial markets. This is illustrated well in Figure 8-3. You can see that for the

20-year period ending on 12/31/2016, the average investor earned less than every investment tracked in the study. They barely earned more than the annual inflation rate!

HOW THE AVERAGE INVESTOR STACKS UP

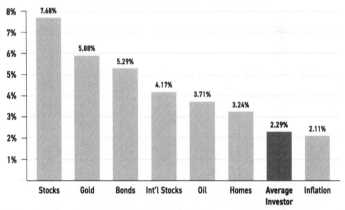

Figure 8-3. How the Average Investor Stacks Up (Source: BlackRock, Investing and Emotions, 2017. Used with permission.)

This underperformance has resulted in a dramatic loss of potential wealth. If you had invested $10,000 in the S&P 500 (the stock market) 20 years ago and left it untouched, your ending wealth would have been just less than $44,000. If you had invested in bonds, you would have ended with a little over $28,000. Instead, the average investor ended up with about $15,700 in their portfolio. Think of how much wealthier all of us would be without riding this emotional roller coaster that causes us to buy high and sell low.

For most investors, losing money hurts more than making money feels good. At least logic (and a little math) helps us understand this better. Let's start with one dollar. If you lose 10 percent, you are left with 90 cents. Now let's say that you earn 10 percent on that 90 cents. How much do you have? You've only gotten back to 99 cents. So how much do you need to earn to recover from a 10 percent loss? 11 percent? Nope. That would only total 99.9 cents. You would need to earn a 12 percent return to break even from a 10 percent loss.

If you lose more than 10 percent, that's where the math gets cruel. A 20 percent loss requires a 25 percent return to break even; a 50 percent loss requires a 100 percent return to break even. The more you lose, the harder it is to make it back to even. That's why your investment strategy must be created and maintained in the sweet spot between too much and too little risk.

Even then, markets sometimes behave in unstable ways. Stock market corrections, which are losses of over 10 percent, happen, on average, every one to three years. Bear markets, which are losses of over 20 percent, happen, on average, every three to five years. Worse yet, the wheels seem to completely fall off the wagon every five to ten years. Yet over long periods of time, stocks have averaged gains of more than 11 percent a year.[24]

However, here's the problem with average returns—the markets rarely earn exactly the average return. They usually earn more or less (sometimes much more or much less) than the average.

For example, if I put my head into a 200-degree oven and placed my feet in a zero-degree bucket of ice, my body temperature would be about 98.6 degrees *on average*. I would also be flatlining and on my way to a hospital. The average doesn't help too much.

Financial, economic, and political events are wildly unpredictable. Even if your average return is expected to be positive, it's important to understand and expect swings—sometimes, violent ones—to occur from time to time.

The next time one of these occurrences happens, you'll remember that these "unpredictable," unforeseen events occur rather predictably. Armed with this knowledge, you are already better prepared to deal with the swirl of negative emotions that will threaten to influence your investing behavior.

---

24 J.P. Morgan Asset Management Market Insights, Guide to the Markets, Range of Stock, Bond, and Blended Total Returns, Annual Total Returns, 1950-2016, April 2017, page 63. https://am.jpmorgan.com/us/en/asset-management/gim/adv/insights/guide-to-the-markets.

The four most dangerous words in investing are "this time it's different," because that is always the argument about why this time the sky really *is* falling. But it's never different. The market goes up, it goes down, and it always goes back up again. It doesn't matter how low the market goes; it has always come back. We just don't know when that will happen.

RETIREMENT MYTH #4

Why should I contribute to the plan when I don't plan on working here very long? If you're thinking this, you've already been working there long enough to qualify to contribute into the plan, which is usually anywhere from one month to one year. It is quite possible that you won't work there much longer, but unless your departure is imminent, begin contributing. You can always transfer whatever you build up there into your next employer's plan.

More often than not, your plans will change, and you end up working there longer than you originally thought—sometimes, much longer. Maybe long enough to miss out on some of the boss's matching contributions. Why give up that free money?

Cost is another consideration. There is much discussion about the cost of investments and the cost of 401(k) plans. It's like anything else; price is what you pay, and value is what you get. The price only becomes an issue if you feel that you have not received value for the products or services you have paid for. This can be broken down into common financial sense in Figure 8-4, because there are only three costs to your 401(k) plan.

Costs for 401(k) plans and the investments within a plan vary from one to another. Be sure to understand all of the costs of your plan, and don't be shy about inquiring with your plan's administrator at your company or the plan provider company. They should be able to explain in plain terms what your total costs are and how they break down between the costs of the investments, recordkeeping, and administration.

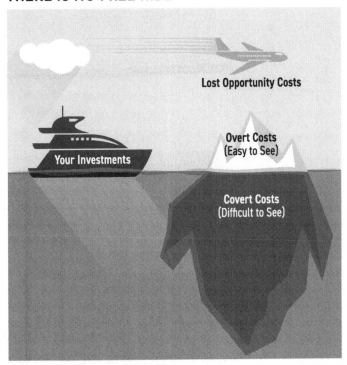

Figure 8-4. There Is No Free Ride (Source: CFS Investment Advisory Services, L.L.C., 2018. Used with permission.)

The first costs are the overt costs, or the costs that are easy to determine. Many of these costs were covert (hidden) but are now overt (plainly seen) due to the recently enacted rule requiring that the plan's fee disclosure notice be given at least once a year to everyone in the plan. You should be receiving this document from your employer or plan provider. These costs include:

- The mutual fund expense ratio (the fee the mutual fund company charges to manage the money)

- General administrative fees, such as the fees the 401(k) company charges for recordkeeping the plan (i.e., providing a website, newsletter, and IRS reporting)
- The investment advisor's fee (for compliance and employee education)

The second costs are the covert costs, or the costs that are hidden or hard to see. These costs include the trading costs of the mutual funds. Mutual fund managers buy and sell stocks and bonds within the mutual fund. This buying and selling generates costs that are very difficult to measure, because they are not required to disclose them as a separate line item.

The third costs are the lost-opportunity costs of the investment choices given to you compared with other similar, lower-cost, and better-performing choices that aren't included.

In other words, this cost is the difference between the return you *get* on your investment and the return you *could have* gotten if a similar but better-performing investment had been available to you within that plan.

For example, if the S&P 500 Index has a 10 percent return, and your similarly invested, large company fund has an 8 percent return, then you have a "lost" 2 percent return on your investment—which is the Index return of 10 percent minus the 8 percent you received on your investment. Over time, this "lost opportunity cost" can add up to tens or hundreds of thousands of dollars.

Understand what investment risk means to you. Understand your emotions and overcome them, as rash decisions make it difficult to succeed. Understand the costs of investing.

An old Irish proverb says, "Worry is interest paid on a debt not yet incurred." Spend less time focusing on the things you can't control, such as the investment markets, interest rates, inflation, and political, economic, and financial events. We don't know when corrections, bear markets, and crises will occur.

Spend time focusing on what you can control—your emotions, discipline, and time frame. It is powerful to know that when you experience the next crisis, you will remember that like any storm, this too shall pass.

Figure 8-5 sums this up well. It's called the Common Financial Sense Knowledge Matrix, and we use it to remind ourselves how to categorize any issue that comes up.

If something is unknowable and unimportant, who cares what the issue is? After all, it is both unimportant *and* unknowable, and it will have very little impact on your life.

On the other hand, any information that's knowable but unimportant is noise—nothing more and nothing less.

Too much of what creeps into our heads every day is noise. News can occupy much of this space. You read or hear it and it seems important, so you start to worry about it. Take a step back and ask yourself, "Is this important? How does this affect my life?"

COMMON FINANCIAL SENSE KNOWLEDGE MATRIX

	Unknowable	Knowable
Unimportant	Who Cares?	Noise
Important	Worry	Common Financial Sense

Figure 8-5. Common Financial Sense Knowledge Matrix (Source: CFS Investment Advisory Services, L.L.C., 2018. Used with permission.)

If something is unknowable and important, the only thing created is worry. You know it's important, but you don't know the answer.

No matter how important, worrying over anything that is unknowable is a terrible waste of energy that could negatively affect your emotional, physical, and financial health. We see many people spending too much time in this quadrant. Consequently, they spend a great deal of time worrying instead of focusing on things that are knowable and important.

If information is knowable and important, then you must learn enough about the situation to behave logically and competently. This is where you should spend the majority of your time, because this is where you have the greatest opportunity to control the outcome and create a better life for yourself and your family. This is what we call common financial sense.

INVEST WITH THE RIGHT ATTITUDE

⊘ **Focus intently on the things you can control.**

⊘ **Don't worry about things you have no control over.**

⊘ **Learn from the mistakes of others and "rent" the experience for free from them.**

CHAPTER NINE

SIMPLE STEPS TO HELP YOU SUCCEED

"It ain't what you don't know that gets you into trouble. It's what you know for sure that just ain't so."

MARK TWAIN

If you are unsure whether to participate in your employer's 401(k) plan or invest on your own, please remember that it is almost always in your favor to participate in the 401(k) plan. Let's look into this a little further.

Figure 9-1 illustrates some of the choices that Sarah has. She is earning $45,000 a year and is currently unmarried (marital status needs to be assumed to calculate the effect of current income taxes).

Sarah would like to save 6 percent of her salary, or

$2,700 a year. Using the 2018 IRS tax tables, she will have a tax due of approximately $3,770 after taking the standard deduction and personal exemption amounts. After setting aside $2,700 for savings or investment in Scenario A, Sarah has about $38,530 in spendable income for the year.

SAVING WITH PRE-TAX DOLLARS INCREASES AFTER-TAX SPENDABLE INCOME

 This is Sarah. Sarah does not currently participate in her employer-sponsored retirement plan. However, she is looking to start saving for her retirement. Sarah would like to save $2,700 this year but isn't sure if she should A) open her own investment account with money from her bank account or B) contribute to her company's 401(k) plan directly from her paycheck. The two scenarios illustrated below show how Sarah's spendable income is affected by her method of saving.

Scenario A
Sarah invests the $2,700 directly from her checking account.

Tax Calculation

Total Income	$45,000.00
Standard Deduction	$(12,000.00)
Taxable Income	$33,000.00
Taxes Due	**$(3,769.50)**

Spendable Income Calculation

Total Income	$45,000.00
Taxes Due	$(3,769.50)
Net Income	$41,230.50
Savings	$(2,700.00)
Spendable Income	**$38,530.50**

Scenario B
Sarah enrolls in her company's 401(k) plan and has her $2,700 deducted directly from her paycheck before taxes are calculated.

Tax Calculation

Total Income	$45,000.00
401(k) Contribution	$(2,700.00)
Standard Deduction	$(12,000.00)
Taxable Income	$30,300.00
Taxes Due	**$(3,445.50)**

Spendable Income Calculation

Total Income	$45,000.00
401(k) Contribution	$(2,700.00)
Taxes Due	$(3,445.50)
Spendable Income	**$38,854.50**

Scenario B, enrolling in her company's 401(k) plan, gives Sarah $324.00 more to spend each year than Scenario A.

Figure 9-1. Saving with Pre-Tax Dollars Increases After-Tax Spendable Income (Source: CFS Investment Advisory Services, L.L.C., 2018. Used with permission.)

On the other hand, if she chooses Scenario B and contributes $2,700 to her 401(k) account, her taxes due will be approximately $3,446, with $38,854.50 in spendable income.

By investing in her 401(k), Sarah enjoys an increase of over $320 in spendable income. Please compare your own situation with current tax rules, but like Sarah, you will usually come out ahead by contributing to your 401(k) plan.

Another advantage of investing through your 401(k) plan is that contributions are made by deductions directly from your paycheck. The money that gets invested comes right off the top of your check before you get paid. It's out of sight and out of mind.

Not only that, but by having your contribution made through payroll deduction, the same amount of money is being invested at regular intervals at every pay period throughout the year. Investing this way, over regular intervals throughout the year, is also referred to as *dollar cost averaging*.

One terrific way to mitigate the risk of investing over time is by investing in the dollar cost averaging method. This method is straightforward in that it just requires the discipline to invest the same amount of money at the same regular intervals over time. Discipline is required because when the markets are performing poorly, your instinct may be to change where your funds are invested or to stop investing altogether.

This is one of the ironies of investing. When the markets go down, the major publicly traded companies have gone on sale. Yet no one wants to invest during the sale. The average individual investor waits until the sale is over, and markets have gone back up before investing again. Warren Buffett, one of the best investors in our lifetime, once said, "You make most of your money in a bad market; you just don't realize it at the time."

Like the famous fable of the tortoise and the hare, slow and steady wins the race. You must have willpower to successfully invest the dollar cost averaging way. The 401(k) plan is one of the easiest and best ways to accomplish this, because your investments are being made at regular intervals when your contribution is deducted from your check each pay cycle. Unless you have recently made a change to the amount you contribute, the amount remains the same, as well.

DOLLAR COST AVERAGING CAN HELP YOU

You have $1,440 to invest.
You can choose to invest it all at once in one lump sum, or invest $120/month for 12 months.

Figure 9-2. Dollar Cost Averaging Can Help You (Source: CFS Investment Advisory Services, L.L.C., 2018. Used with permission.)

Figure 9-2 compares a $1,440 investment made once at the beginning of the year versus investing $120 a month on the first day of each month of the year. In both cases, you've invested the same amount of money during the year. However, you have different results.

By investing the same amount of money over the regular intervals, you have been able to use the ups and downs of the market to your advantage. Some months you bought more shares, and other months you bought fewer shares. By averaging the cost of your investments over the entire year, you have taken advantage of the price fluctuations that occur over time.

Investing regular amounts steadily over time (dollar cost averaging) may lower your average per-share cost. Remember that periodic investment ideas such as this cannot guarantee a profit or protect against loss in a declining market. Rather than looking for quick gains, dollar cost averaging is a long-term strategy involving continuous investing, regardless of fluctuating price levels. That's why it is well suited to a 401(k) investor. Payroll deductions turn money over to your account steadily throughout the year, allowing the benefit of periodically lower per-share costs alongside the relative stability of a long-term return.

Another advantage of investing through your 401(k) plan is that the majority of the money you will have in your account when you retire will come from tax-deferred compounding, not your contributions.

Let's look at the three employees that work at the same company in Figure 9-3. Their names are Lisa, Bob, and Joe. Lisa and Bob are both 25 and Joe is 42. We will assume all three will retire at age 65, and the money invested in their 401(k) accounts will earn 7 percent a year.

Lisa and Bob invest $250 a month into their 401(k) accounts, but Bob stops in ten years at age 35 while Lisa continues until age 65.

Joe is a little older and has only 23 years to invest, so he saves $500 a month until age 65.

Lisa ends up with the largest balance. This makes sense, of course, because she put the most into her account. But Bob and Joe ended up with similar amounts, even though Joe had to save much more money to get there.

LET TIME AND COMPOUNDING WORK FOR YOU

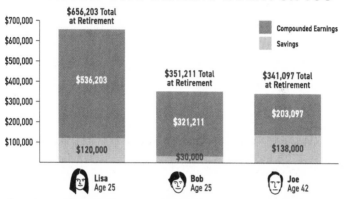

Figure 9-3. Let Time and Compounding Work for You (Source: CFS Investment Advisory Services, L.L.C., 2018. Used with permission.)

Assumptions: Lisa begins saving for retirement at age 25. She saves $250 per month for 40 years until she reaches retirement at age 65. Bob also begins saving for his retirement at age 25, but only saves $250 per month for 10 years and then lets his account grow for the next 30 years, until he reaches retirement at age 65. Joe does not begin saving for his retirement until he is 42, but he saves $500 per month for 23 years, until he retires at age 65. All accounts have an assumed 7 percent annual rate of return.

The most surprising part of this exercise is that most of their account values came from tax-deferred compounding, not the amount they saved.

Lisa earned over $530,000 on her contribution of $120,000 for a total of over $650,000. Bob also earned most of his money through the tax-deferred compounding, turning his $30,000 into over $350,000. Even Joe did well, earning over $200,000 of his total $340,000 from tax-deferred compounding.

Of course, the example here of a 7 percent investment performance does not represent the return of any specific investment and doesn't guarantee any future rate of return.

RETIREMENT MYTH #5

Sometimes thinking about your retirement is so scary to you that you put up a force field around yourself and say something clever like, "I'm too busy to be bothered." Too busy? There is no reason you can't carve out a little time now to invest in yourself and your future.

Have a brief conversation with your 401(k) plan's investment advisor and enlist his or her support. They are there to help you and should be eager and able to assist anyone who shows interest or who has questions about how to proceed from whatever point you're at.

INVEST WITH DETERMINATION

⊘ Tax-deferred savings through your 401(k) plan is an efficient way to save for retirement.

⊘ Dollar cost averaging can be a potent way to lessen the effects of stock market volatility.

⊘ Stay determined and use these ideas to help you stay on track.

CHAPTER TEN

HOW SHOULD I INVEST?

"Good judgment is the result of experience and experience is the result of bad judgment."

MARK TWAIN

Have you ever watched a business program on one of the cable television networks when the stock market was the topic of discussion? You see experts moving their lips and words are coming out of their mouths. As you try to focus on what they're saying, it almost actually sounds like they are making sense.

But then you zero in on their words, and you can't understand what they're talking about. That's because they're conversing in "Financialese." Although similar to English, it's a language all its own.

This endless babbling is deliberately done to confuse and

frustrate you. The message these shows hope to deliver is that you need to watch their program to comprehend these words of wisdom. This much is true: if they keep making it seem confusing and hard to understand, then it will certainly be more difficult for you to figure any of this out for yourself.

There is a way to explain stocks in a simple but not over-simplified way. That sure would help us all! Of course, some outlets wouldn't like this, because they would be left with lots of dead air to fill every day.

We don't need Financialese. Let's continue with more common financial sense.

What is a stock? Stock is partial ownership of a company that is traded in units called *shares*.

There are over 3,500 different companies whose shares trade on a major stock exchange in this country. That's an awful lot of possibilities to consider. That said, there are only nine kinds of stocks you can buy, broken down by three types and sizes, as shown in Figure 10-1.

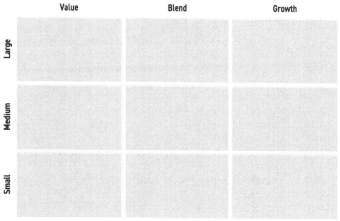

Figure 10-1.

The three general types of stocks are *value*, *growth*, and a *blend* of the two.

Value companies make products and services in industries or sectors that are more fully developed. The market size is usually better understood, but the company is trying to gain the biggest share of that known market. A value company can also be a growth company that falls on hard times and sells for a price that is a "better value."

Growth companies produce goods and services in industries or sectors that are still growing. The total size of the market for those goods and services may not be known yet because it's still growing.

Blend companies have characteristics of both growth and value companies. They have some products or services in markets that are growing but also have some that are in more mature markets. You will encounter the blended type of investment in your 401(k) retirement plan, and it will most likely consist of mutual funds that invest in both growth and value companies.

Now, each of these three types of companies comes in three different general sizes: large, medium, and small. When each variable is applied, it creates nine different types of stocks.

Large companies are usually $10 billion or larger in size.

Medium companies are usually between $2 to $10 billion.

Small companies are usually less than $2 billion.

These billions are market *capitalization* and are calculated by multiplying the number of shares a company has outstanding by the company's stock price per share. That's why the term *cap* (as in large cap, mid cap, or small cap) gets thrown in sometimes when there's a discussion about stocks.

A bond is a unit of debt issued by federal, state, and local governments. Corporations can also issue bonds. When you invest in a bond, you are lending money to that government entity or corporation, which will be paid back to you at a set date in the future. Bonds can vary in length up to 30 years, sometimes even longer. You are paid a set amount of interest on a regular basis as payment for lending the money.

Think of it like this: stock investing is ownership, and bond investing is "loanership."

Let's apply this in a practical way. We have seen that investment companies group stocks and/or bonds into different buckets based on types or sizes. Sometimes, they also group stocks together because they are in the same or similar industry. These buckets are called mutual funds.

Mutual funds allow you to pool your money with other investors into one larger amount, so the investment companies can put together a group of securities they hope will do well when invested together. Think of it as a bucket of money where professional money managers buy and sell stocks and bonds for the investors in the mutual fund.

There are two major schools of thought about investing today: passive management vs. active management.

Passively managed mutual funds, better known as index funds, are primarily run by computer programs that replicate the stock market index or bond market index that the fund is based on. Passive managers believe that by the time you get done paying for the active money manager and research, you have lost any advantage a good manager has and that you will actually underperform the market if you're unfortunate enough to pick a poorly managed mutual fund.

Active money management believes that with good research, patience, and discipline, you can do better than the stock or bond market index. Actively managed mutual funds are managed by people who are grouping types and sizes of stocks by doing research and picking the stocks they feel are going to do well.

Each school has its proponents and naysayers. We don't pick sides because we believe that there is no one type, style, size, or strategy for all seasons. Because there are no absolutes, we like to cover as many bases as the 401(k) plan investment menu will allow.

The best way to cover those bases is to understand the investment menu itself. The enrollment form provides you with a long list of mutual funds, but no context from which you can best understand how to choose which combination may be most suited to your needs. Usually, the investment menu will have a choice of actively managed funds and passively managed index funds.

Three important skills will help you pick the most suitable combination.

First, gain at least a basic understanding of how these investments work in different investment environments. Next, find the time necessary to monitor your choices. Lastly, have the inclination to want to pay attention to all of this with the limited amount of free time you have.

Some people treat investing like a hobby, so they enjoy reading and researching different mutual funds and their managers. However, few people are inclined to learn and maintain the skills necessary to put together their own portfolio of funds.

RETIREMENT MYTH #6

"It is better to be safe than sorry." It's that thinking which may also leave you without enough money in retirement. People tend to invest too conservatively throughout their lifetime. This is a particularly bad setback if you invest too conservatively when you're still young, because you miss out on all of the compounding that you benefit from in the early years of 401(k) contributions.

The stock market is one of the most ironic markets there is. That's because the stock market has no short-term truths. On any given day, the stock market may go up or down. It is completely random from day to day. So short term, it can be a very risky place to invest. However, over very long periods of time (20, 30, or 40 years), the stock market tends only to go up. That's the long-term truth. Take another look at Figure 8-1, The Range of Stock, Bond, and Blended Total Returns in Chapter Eight to review the historical evidence.

The stock market is also one of the most counterintuitive markets that you'll find anywhere. If you want to buy a shirt or blouse, you go to the store and buy it. A month or two later, you learn that the store has a big sale going on, 40 percent off! You go back to the store and buy more. You call or text a friend and ask them if they would like to buy some because there's a great sale going on. Of course, you want to get in on the deal before the price goes back to its usual price. That's a pretty familiar scene.

What happens when you want to invest? Let's say that you invest $1,000 in your mutual fund when its cost is $20 a share. A month or two later, you hear that the stock market has gone down, you look at your account, and you are shocked to see that the value has gone down 40 percent! The price of your fund has gone down to $12 a share. You "lost" $400!

You want to sell your shares, and you call your friend who also invested in the fund when you did, and you both sell, taking the loss. But you *should* want to buy more because your investment and the stock market overall is on sale.

Is that your inclination, though? Of course not.

That's what is so counterintuitive. If you liked the fund at $20 a share and nothing has happened to it, then you should really like the fund at $12 a share and buy more. However, we don't—we sell.

It seems as though this is the average person's experience with investing: to buy high and then sell low. Understanding that the stock market is ironic and counterintuitive is an important concept that can help you invest successfully. These are important principles that allow you to keep your cool while everyone else around you loses theirs. It also gives you the emotional strength to maintain the discipline not only to stay invested but also to invest more as the market goes down.

Now that you have a better understanding of the difference between a stock (share of a company) and a bond (unit of debt), as well as the nine different types of stocks (value, growth, and blend in large, medium, and small cap sizes), you are ready to build an investment portfolio.

Building a portfolio involves the idea of asset allocation. Asset allocation is a fancy way of saying, "Don't put all of your eggs in one basket." It's the way to diversify your portfolio so that you can balance out your goals, risk tolerance, and investment time horizon. It is deciding how much you want to put into stocks, bonds, and money markets. Research has shown that this is the most important decision that you can make. It is much more important than trying to pick which investment to put your money in.

The first step to asset allocation is deciding how much to put into growth investments (stocks), income investments (bonds), and safe investments (money markets and stable value funds).

If you are a young investor, then your retirement goals are very long-term. You may be working 30 or 40 years, so your time horizon is long. You may want to build a portfolio for long-term growth that has the majority of the investments in stocks. If you are in your 50s or older, then your time horizon is shorter, so you may want to put more of your money in less risky investments like bonds, money markets, and stable value funds.

Once you decide on the percentages between stocks, bonds, and money markets, then you need to decide what kinds of stocks and bonds to invest in.

Remember the nine different types of stocks? To properly allocate your account, you should have money in each of these types of stocks because they all act differently at different times throughout the business cycle. Sometimes growth companies outperform value companies. Sometimes large companies outperform small- and medium-sized companies.

You also need to decide how much money you want to put into international stocks and bonds, because sometimes, international stocks and bonds outperform US stocks and bonds.

Once you have decided on your asset allocation, you should then rebalance your account at least once a year. Rebalancing is bringing your asset allocation back to where you want it.

Consider this: Suppose you decide that you want 50 percent of your money in stocks and 50 percent of your money in bonds. Now let's assume that the stock market goes up by 10 percent. You made money!

But now you have 55 percent in stocks and only 45 percent in bonds. Your asset allocation has changed. Your portfolio is riskier because you have 55 percent in stocks, not the 50 percent you decided upon.

When you rebalance, you take your profit in the stocks by selling them and buying bonds so that your asset allocation is back to 50 percent stocks and 50 percent bonds, as shown in Figure 10-2.

PORTFOLIO REBALANCING

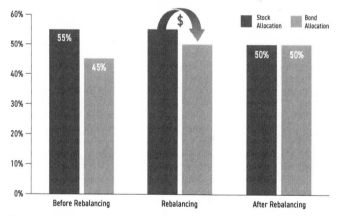

Figure 10-2. Portfolio Rebalancing (Source: CFS Investment Advisory Services, L.L.C., 2018. Used with permission.)

Conversely, let's think about your 50 percent stock and 50 percent bond portfolio in a different way. Let's now assume that the stock market goes down by 10 percent. Now you have 45 percent in stocks and 55 percent in bonds. Your asset allocation is too conservative.

When you rebalance, you sell some of your bonds and buy back into the stock market to get back to 50 percent stocks and 50 percent bonds. Rebalancing forces you to buy low and sell high with parts of the portfolio.

If all of this sounds like we're speaking a foreign language and you're really confused, the good news is that most 401(k) investment menus have a third group of investments to choose from. Not surprisingly, these are called *managed portfolios.*

The main advantage of managed portfolios is that the fund manager chooses the mix of all the funds you invest in (the asset allocation). The manager determines the percentage of large, midsize, and small companies, as well as the mix of growth and value styles. Furthermore, they determine the mix between stocks and bonds.

Simply put, you are allowing the fund manager to make all of the asset allocation decisions within one investment.

Managed portfolios are either risk-based or age-based. Risk-based portfolios maintain a similar amount of risk over time. They are usually described as conservative, moderate, or aggressive so you can better understand how much risk one portfolio has as compared with another. You determine how much risk you want to take, and the fund maintains that level of risk throughout the amount of time you remain invested in the fund. As you get older, you decide if you would like to reduce the amount of risk you want to take and make changes accordingly.

Age-based managed portfolios are better known as target-date funds or lifecycle funds. Target-date mutual fund managers also pick all the investments in the portfolio. Like risk-based funds, target-date funds are very well diversified among many kinds of investments. Instead of managing the portfolio based on a steady amount of risk, target-date funds reduce the amount of risk as you get closer to your retirement age.

Target-date mutual funds are usually classified in five-year increments based on the year you want to retire (2020, 2025, 2030, etc.). If you have many years until retirement, you may want to choose a 2060 fund, because the year 2060 is quite a long time into the future.

The fund manager will invest in a more aggressive mix of investments because you have many years until you retire. If you are near retirement, you may want to choose a 2020 fund because the manager is managing the portfolio based on the average investor's risk profile of someone who will retire in the year 2020. These funds tend to have more conservative investments because they assume that you will be retiring in or around the year 2020.

By allowing the professionals to determine the mix of investments and monitor their progress, you are freed up to channel your energies into other activities that you may find more productive.

Always remember there is no one perfect set of investments, there are no guarantees that you will reach your goals, and investing this way certainly does not prevent loss. It does provide you with peace of mind, though, because when the investment markets go down, as they all eventually and temporarily do, you don't have to worry about tinkering with your investment choices.

What kind of investor are you? Do you have the skills? Do you have the desire and time to devote to these activities?

If you have the skills, desire, and time, you should consider doing it yourself. If not, you should think about delegating these decisions to the managed portfolios and use the risk-based or target-date funds your plan offers.

There are many sources of help. You can always ask the retirement plan investment advisor for assistance; a personal financial planner can also be a valuable counselor. Keep asking questions until you are comfortable with the answers. Most importantly, don't let your lack of understanding about this subject prevent you from contributing and profiting from your retirement plan.

INVEST WITH PATIENCE

⊘ Investing for the long term doesn't have to be confusing even though the system appears confusing.

⊘ Do not get distracted by all of the financial noise out there. It's everywhere, and it's loud.

⊘ The one single trait that EVERY successful investor has is patience.

CHAPTER ELEVEN

THE ROTH 401(K) OPTION

"The only difference between death and taxes is that death doesn't get worse every time Congress meets."

WILL ROGERS

After careful consideration, you have made many important decisions to get to this point. But you're not done yet. You still need to consider choosing whether to invest in a traditional 401(k) or a Roth 401(k). Although the Roth 401(k) has been around for a long time, we still find that people are confused by the nuances that make it different from the traditional 401(k).

No one likes paying taxes. However, you may be able to control when you pay some of them, depending on which 401(k) choice you make. What is the difference between the Roth 401(k) and a traditional 401(k)? The answer to that question lies in another question. When do you want to pay your income taxes: now or at retirement?

The traditional 401(k) is tax deductible when you contribute. If you contribute $5,000 a year, and if you are in a 20 percent tax bracket, you save $1,000 a year in income taxes. The money goes into your account before taxes are calculated; in effect, the government is subsidizing your account by the tax deduction. $5,000 goes into the account, but only $4,000 comes out of your paycheck. When you retire, all the money you take out of your 401(k) account is counted as taxable income. Most people don't take a lump sum distribution because the income taxes would be too high. Instead, they usually take a monthly or annual distribution over their lifetime and pay the income taxes when the money comes out.

The Roth 401(k) is not tax deductible when you make your contributions. If you make a $5,000 a year contribution, $5,000 a year comes out of your paycheck. You do not get the income tax savings. So, why would anyone prefer it? Because when you take the money out at retirement, it all comes out income tax-free. Think about that for a moment. Tax-free income when you need it the most—at retirement, when you no longer have a paycheck. Do you want to pay the extra income taxes now when you are working or at retirement when you no longer have a paycheck?

Let's look at the numbers. If you are 25 and contribute $5,000 a year to your 401(k) plan, and if it earns 7 percent a year over 40 years, you will have nearly $1,000,000 in the account.

If you made the contributions pre-tax, you would have saved about $1,000 a year in income taxes (assuming you are in a 20 percent tax bracket—talk to your tax advisor to see if you would save more or less based on your income tax bracket).

Over those 40 years, you would have saved $1,000 every year, for a total of $40,000 in income taxes. But at retirement, your $1,000,000 retirement account is fully taxable.

If you withdrew $50,000 a year, all $50,000 would be added to your taxable income, and you would pay income taxes on it. If you are still in a 20 percent tax bracket, you will pay $10,000 a year in income taxes on the $50,000 distribution.

Instead, if you contribute the $5,000 a year into the Roth 401(k), you would not save the $1,000 a year in income taxes *but* the $1,000,000 in your account could be withdrawn income tax-free.

In other words, when you take an annual withdrawal of $50,000 a year in retirement, you will pay no income taxes on the money! To qualify for the tax-free benefit, your Roth 401(k) must be in existence for at least five years. This example holds true at different ages and different tax brackets.

Talk to your tax advisor about the benefits of the Roth 401(k). Keep in mind that this doesn't have to be an either/or decision. You can make contributions to both your traditional 401(k) and to your Roth 401(k) accounts. Just be sure to remember not to exceed the total limits of $18,500 a year if you are under age 50 and $24,500 a year if you are age 50 or older. These are the same limits applicable to traditional 401(k) contributions.

The question remains: When do you want to pay your income taxes? Now or at retirement?

BE OPPORTUNISTIC

⊘ **Carefully consider whether the Roth 401(k) option is for you.**

⊘ **Make the current tax laws work for you.**

CHAPTER TWELVE

THE EMPLOYER MATCH

"Always treat your employees exactly as you want them to treat your best customers."

STEPHEN R. COVEY

Hopefully, you work for a company that offers a matching contribution to further assist in your retirement planning. The employer matching contribution is an amount of money that the company sets aside for you in your 401(k) plan account. The amount of money put into your account is based on a specific method, also known as the *matching formula*.

The matching formula is usually expressed as a percentage of how much you are contributing to the plan. For example, a popular matching formula is 50 percent of the first 6 percent. In English, that means that the company will make a matching contribution of 50 cents into your account for every dollar you put away to a maximum of 6 percent.

IF YOU CONTRIBUTE:	THE COMPANY CONTRIBUTES:
1%	0.5%
2%	1.0%
3%	1.5%
4%	2.0%
5%	2.5%
6%	3.0%
Any amount higher than 6%	3.0%

In this example, the matching formula means that this company will contribute toward your retirement, but it caps out at 3 percent. It will not contribute any amount above that. Always understand what your company's matching formula is. It can change over the years, so make sure you keep up to date with it.

A common mistake we see is that people only invest enough to capture the company match and nothing more. The problem is that if you stop at that point, you will still be short of an account balance high enough to provide you with the income you'll need in retirement. You should invest beyond the matching formula maximum, because it increases the chance that you'll save enough for retirement.

The biggest mistake we see is not contributing at all. If your company matches your contribution in any way, why aren't you contributing? You're leaving free money—the boss's free money—on the table. Using the example above, you could be leaving 3 percent of your pay behind. That's 3 percent that your company is offering you as an incentive to help you help yourself in saving for retirement. What would happen if you asked for a 3 percent raise? If you're not contributing, you're leaving that 3 percent raise behind.

RETIREMENT MYTH #7

You decide that you're not going to invest in your retirement plan because your employer isn't making a matching contribution. A company that offers a match of any kind is generous in assisting you to save for retirement and is certainly a terrific benefit to have, but it is only going to provide a portion of the amount you'll need later on.

If your employer doesn't offer a matching contribution, you will still need money to live on in retirement. Even if you are saving in other ways, you're going to have to save a little more. It doesn't mean that you should abandon this tool for retirement just because your company doesn't contribute to the plan.

The rate of return on your 401(k) plan investments in these cases is irrelevant. Why? Because it is the alternative rate of return that matters. What is the alternative rate of return you earn if you don't invest into your 401(k) plan? Zero!

Simply put, by contributing regularly, increasing the amount you contribute over time, and having the discipline to remain invested through the years will provide you with a much larger retirement plan outcome. That outcome is what provides you with the income you'll need to live on. Of course, you will be monitoring your progress over time, so your investments should do fine.

When your company offers a match in your retirement account, it does so for a number of reasons. The matching contribution is an employee benefit to you for working there. It is part of your compensation and benefits package. Therefore, the company wants to remain competitive in the workplace. It wants to reward those who save for their retirement, and it wants to reward employees who have been working there a long time.

A well-thought-out matching program is a key component of fostering long-term loyalty with you. That said, the company matching contribution usually comes with a string attached. That string is called a *vesting schedule*, and vesting represents how much of the money is yours to keep. The longer you've been employed there, the more you get to accumulate. There are a few different vesting schedules, but here is a common one that we often see.

IF YOU HAVE BEEN AT THE COMPANY:	PERCENT OF MATCH YOU ARE VESTED IN:
Less than 2 Years	0%
2 Years but less than 3 Years	20%
3 Years but less than 4 Years	40%
4 Years but less than 5 Years	60%
5 Years but less than 6 Years	80%
6 Years or more	100%

In this illustration, someone who has been working there three years, but less than four years is 40 percent vested in the company's matching contribution. That means that if you were to leave the company, you would be entitled to take 100 percent of your contributions and 40 percent of the money that the company set aside for you. If you leave after working there for over six years, you are entitled to take 100 percent of the employer matching portion of your account and, of course, all of your contributions.

Remember that you are always 100 percent vested in all of the contributions you make into your 401(k) retirement plan account. After all, it was your money that you put into the account, so you always retain 100 percent ownership of it.

Some 401(k) retirement plans are known as *safe harbor* plans. They provide a required, employer-paid contribution or match to your retirement plan account within IRS safe harbor laws. The matching formulas differ, but you are always 100 percent immediately vested in the employer safe harbor contribution as soon as you are eligible to receive it.

INVEST USING TEAMWORK

⊘ Don't leave company money on the table. It's a free raise!

⊘ Maximize your 401(k) investment so you will gather all of your employer's matching contribution.

⊘ Don't stop there though, because the employer match usually stops at a lower percentage than you'll need to plan for.

⊘ Teaming up with your employer will get you there quicker than by yourself.

CHAPTER THIRTEEN

MONITORING YOUR PROGRESS

"Slow and steady wins the race."

AESOP

There are different ways to measure your progress and the success of your 401(k) investment account over time. One of the more popular measurements is the comparison of your 401(k) account's investment return against the return of broad market benchmarks such as the S&P 500 or the Dow Jones Industrial Average indexes.

This is inappropriate because none of these benchmarks ever retire. None will ever be expected to pay out a reliable retirement income. None are aware of your personal needs, time frames or appetite for risk. Raw return percentages don't necessarily mean that you have been successful either.

After all, you may earn a 100 percent return in your 401(k) account, but if all that does is increase your total account at retirement from $10,000 to $20,000, you're still probably not going to have enough to last you for very long.

A better and more appropriate way to measure your progress is to compare your account balance against your long-term retirement goals. A good way to do this is to use the retirement planning calculator tool that your 401(k) plan provider has set up for you on their website.

This calculator should be very useful in understanding many things. First, you should be able to determine how much money you'll need to save before you retire. Then you'll be able to determine how much money you're on pace to have at retirement. Finally, you'll be able to measure the shortfall or gap between where you are headed and where you need to get. This becomes the road map to measure your progress over time as adjustments are made along the way.

A good calculator will also allow you to incorporate assumptions about your future potential Social Security retirement benefits, any outside investments you may have, and any retirement account balances your significant other has as well. This will allow you to get a more complete picture of your situation, which, in turn, will allow you to design a more realistic model.

This calculator gives you a track to run on. It allows you to set, monitor, and meet your retirement planning goals along the way. It is a vital tool in keeping pace with knowing how much money to contribute to your plan account. If you don't know how to use the calculator, ask your plan's investment advisor for help or call the retirement company that is managing the plan. You are paying for help—you should use the help.

RETIREMENT MYTH #8

Another popular myth is the belief that your contributions will not amount to much by the time you retire. This is accepting defeat before you've attempted success. The fact is that the younger you are, the more the money will come from the returns of the investments, not the contributions themselves.

Let's graph the results of the following scenario: let's assume that you start to contribute into your 401(k) plan account at age 25.

At that time, you're earning a salary of $45,000 a year. You're going to contribute 6 percent of your income in the first year and will increase that amount by 1 percent a year until you hit the current maximum allowed by current law ($18,500 a year if age 49 or younger and $24,500 a year if age 50 or older). We're also going to assume that you'll receive salary increases of 3 percent a year and that you'll earn 7 percent a year on your investments in the plan. Lastly, we assume that there is no employer match for this plan. Now let's take a look at Figure 13-1.

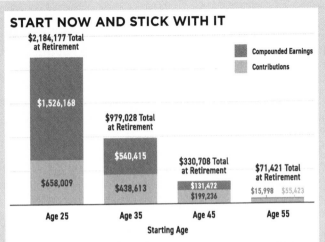

START NOW AND STICK WITH IT

Compounded Earnings
Contributions

$2,184,177 Total at Retirement
$1,526,168
$658,009

$979,028 Total at Retirement
$540,415
$438,613

$330,708 Total at Retirement
$131,472
$199,236

$71,421 Total at Retirement
$15,998 $55,423

Age 25   Age 35   Age 45   Age 55

Starting Age

Figure 13-1. Start Now and Stick With It (Source: CFS Investment Advisory Services, L.L.C., 2018. Used with permission.)

Assumptions: Participant's salary is $45,000 in Year 1. Each year his or her salary increases by 3 percent. The participant starts with a contribution of 6 percent of his or her salary and increases 1 percent each year until the current contribution, plus the catch-up limit, is reached. The investment portfolio has an assumed rate of return of 7 percent per year. All assumptions remain constant until participant's retirement at age 65.

From age 25 to age 65, you will have contributed $658,009 to your 401(k) plan account, and it will grow to $2,184,177 at age 65. Almost 70 percent of that—over $1.5 million dollars—comes from the compounding of your account, not the amount you put in.

You still enjoy the benefits of compounding when you start at older ages too. If you start contributing at age 35, over 55 percent of your total at age 65 is from the compounding of your returns.

If you begin at age 45, almost 40 percent of your retirement benefit accumulates from compounding. Even if you wait until age 55 to go ahead with it, over 22 percent of your total return comes from the compounding of your account.

The most important thing to remember is that no matter when you begin or at what amount, compounding your contributions will bring you much closer to your goal than you think.

The cost of waiting to start putting money into your 401(k) plan is extremely high. Even worse, there are no do-overs!

Let's illustrate this in two different ways. First, let's review Figure 13-2. You start saving at age 25 and contribute $2,000 a year for 40 years until age 65. Let's also assume that you won't increase the annual amount you put into your 401(k) account during your entire career. Lastly, assume that you will earn 7 percent a year on your account balance.

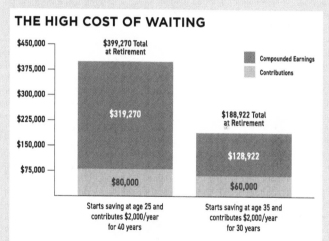

Figure 13-2. The High Cost of Waiting (Source: CFS Investment Advisory Services, L.L.C., 2018. Used with permission.)

Assumptions: 7 percent annual rate of return and tax-deferred compounding.

You will have about $400,000 at age 65. If you wait ten years and invest the same way, $2,000 a year for the remaining 30 years until retirement, and earn 7 percent a year, you end up with less than half the amount—about $189,000. Waiting ten years to fund your 401(k) account will cost you more than $210,000.

Let's look at it another way in Figure 13-3. This time we'll assume that you will contribute $3,000 a year into your 401(k) plan account and it will earn 7 percent a year.

No matter when you begin, you will have more money if you start young. Beginning at age 25, your investments will grow to nearly $600,000 at age 65. If you wait just two years to start at age 27, you will have over $80,000 less at age 65. The two-year delays from ages 35, 45, and 55 cost you plenty as well.

Start early and stick with it.

HOW MUCH DOES WAITING TO SAVE REALLY COST?

Figure 13-3. How Much Does Waiting to Save Really Cost? (Source: CFS Investment Advisory Services, L.L.C., 2018. Used with permission.)

Assumptions: Annual contribution of $3,000 earning a 7 percent rate of return and tax-deferred compounding. All assumptions remain constant until participant's retirement at age 65.

EXECUTE YOUR STRATEGY

⊘ Start your investing right now; even a 1 percent difference makes a big difference over time.

⊘ Increase your 401(k) investment contribution percentage every year until you hit the maximum or at least 15 percent of your income.

⊘ The tortoise wins this race, not the hare—but you have to start the race.

⊘ Execution is key. You have planned, you're making good investment decisions, and now you must monitor the progress toward your financial goals.

CHAPTER FOURTEEN

ACHIEVE FINANCIAL WELLNESS

"You've got to be very careful if you don't know where you are going, because you might not get there."

YOGI BERRA

No matter how old you are, now is the time to take the subject of your retirement seriously. That means examining and changing your spending and saving habits. If you are in your 20s, start your retirement planning off right by starting with good habits. Contribute as much as you can into your 401(k) plan and increase that amount by 1 percent a year. Remember that in order to meet your retirement goals, you should set aside at least 10 percent to 15 percent of your salary a year.

In your 20s, it's also the time to establish a good credit record. It's okay to have and use credit cards. After all, it's very important to have good credit so you can borrow for big-ticket items like a car or house. Just be sure not to run up a big balance and charge only what you can pay off every month. Use a cash back card and budget those savings for your retirement plan as a bonus.

From an investment perspective, use time and diversification to your maximum advantage. Invest in a diversified portfolio that may include some higher-risk investments. That will allow you to get used to riding the ups and downs of the market, which is especially good while you are younger.

In your 30s, you may start to see a lot of competing needs having to be met. That's why it's important to make the most of your excellent retirement savings habits during these years. If you have children, start saving for their college education. You should maintain an "emergency fund" in the bank, consisting of three to six months' of living expenses available in case of a financial emergency or opportunity.

If you have credit card debt, pay off the account that has the highest interest rate and try to pay more than the minimum amount due every month so it can be paid off quicker. Then pay down the next highest interest rate card, and so on, until you are debt-free or close to it. Avoid large amounts of debt because they are costly now and to your future. Every dollar going to pay off credit card interest charges is a dollar that can't be available for your other budget items, including your 401(k) contribution.

Just like in your 20s, you should still be thinking about investing for growth, as you have many years before retirement arrives. Make sure you have obtained the proper amounts of life, health, and disability insurance. Be sure to coordinate these coverages with any benefits available to you through your employer.

RETIREMENT MYTH #9

"Borrowing money from my account while I'm working won't really matter in the long run because, after all, I'm paying myself the interest."

Let's take a closer look at that, though. If you take a loan, the fact is that you'll have to pay taxes twice on the same dollars. Here's how.

The first tax occurs when you withdraw the money during retirement. Everyone recognizes that. The second tax occurs when you take a loan. Taking the loan is not a taxable event, but think about the money that you're using to pay back the loan.

It's "after-tax dollars," money that was taxed from your paycheck just to go back into your plan to repay the loan. Not such a great idea after all. Remember that this is a retirement account, not your personal piggy bank.

By the time you reach your 40s, you should have started to accumulate a nice balance in your 401(k) account. Now is the time to begin monitoring your progress. Are you on track to retire and live the way you would like to?

Log in to your retirement plan's website and familiarize yourself with the retirement calculator it uses. The retirement calculator may also be called a *gap analyzer*, because it may point out any gaps you may have in retirement benefit amounts. This is a great way to determine whether there is a gap between your retirement goals and the projected outcome it shows. If it shows a projected shortfall, make the adjustments necessary in your contribution amount so you can meet your goals.

If you haven't already done so, now is the time to maximize your contributions to the plan. As of this writing, you can contribute $18,500 a year into your 401(k) plan. It takes perseverance and discipline to create and manage good savings habits. Continue monitoring the progress toward your retirement financial goals on your plan's retirement calculator. Create a will as well as updating beneficiaries for your 401(k) account and your other assets.

As you enter your 50s, you can start contributing an additional amount into your 401(k) plan, called the *catch-up contribution*, beginning in the year you turn age 50. The current maximum catch-up contribution amount is

$6,000 a year as of this writing, for a total contribution limit of $24,500 a year.

Start modeling your retirement plan in real time. First, estimate your expected living expenses. Next, estimate the amount of money you'll have available each year by analyzing the results from your plan's retirement calculator.

Be sure to add amounts that will be available from other sources, such as Social Security retirement benefits and other savings. Compare your projected expenses against your estimated income from all sources and calculate how long your money should last.

If you are facing a potential shortfall, now is the time to consider an alternative approach to what you're doing.

Figure 14-1. What If There's a Shortfall? (Source: CFS Investment Advisory Services, L.L.C., 2018. Used with permission.)

Figure 14-1 illustrates the three alternatives, none of them too pleasant. You can save more each year, you can work longer than you originally intended, or you can invest more aggressively than you have been. The good news is that very few people will need to do all three things, but corrective steps are needed now.

Go back to your retirement calculator and toggle some of these variables into it and begin to look at some of the available options. Most people find that they can achieve their goals by a combination of two of the three choices.

Either way, it's best to be aware now instead of adopting the ostrich strategy of sticking your head in the sand.

Consult with your retirement plan's investment advisor or your financial planner to better estimate your potential paths and understand what course of action is well-suited for your needs. In your late 50s, consider purchasing long-term care insurance, which you may need as you begin to get older.

In your 60s, it's time to finish your retirement planning and start making plans for retirement. Determine specific strategies to determine how you'll convert your 401(k) plan and other investment accounts into a consistent income stream.

Some strategies include taking systematic withdrawals, interest, and dividends only, or periodic lump sums. Make sure that you have established a sustainable withdrawal rate. Generally, we suggest not withdrawing more than 3 or 4 percent a year for those who retire at full retirement age.

Review your Social Security retirement benefit options carefully, as there are many different combinations of how to collect your benefits. Make sure to maximize your payout as best you can. Apply for Medicare health coverage when you turn age 65.

Don't let others determine where your money and possessions should go when you die. Now is the time to review and update your will, trusts, and estate plan. At a minimum, you should have three legal documents for this purpose:

- A will, which is a document that instructs how your assets are to be distributed among your surviving heirs.
- A power of attorney, which allows someone else to step in on your behalf concerning your financial affairs if you're incapacitated or otherwise unable to make financial decisions for yourself.
- A healthcare proxy, which authorizes someone to act on your behalf for medical issues and decisions.

INVEST WITH PREPARATION

⊘ Sacrificing a little of today is better than sacrificing a lot of tomorrows.

⊘ Live the life you can afford within your means.

⊘ Don't end up at retirement age with a random amount of savings; strategic preparation is necessary.

CHAPTER FIFTEEN

WHEN YOU LEAVE YOUR COMPANY

"Choose a job you love, and you will never have to work a day in your life."

CONFUCIUS

Chances are that you will work for multiple employers over the length of your career. Therefore, it's highly likely that you will need to enroll and contribute to multiple 401(k) plans as well. There are steps you can take to prevent you from ending up with many different 401(k) accounts.

First, let's take a look at the choices you have when you leave your job. You can leave the money in your former employer's plan. The major advantage of leaving it there is that you don't have to do anything and your account can stay where it is. The disadvantage is that you may be charged some of the fees that the company usually pays for but doesn't cover for ex-employees.

You can choose to roll over your 401(k) account to your next employer's plan. You do want to check with the plan administrator of your new plan to find out if you can roll it over immediately, or if you have to wait until you're eligible to participate in the plan to do so. This is convenient because this allows you to keep all of your 401(k) money together in one account.

You can also choose to roll over your 401(k) account into an Individual Retirement Account (IRA). You should arrange for a direct account-to-account transfer. Your personal financial advisor can properly assist you with this transaction. If you choose an IRA, you can move the account back into a future employer's 401(k) plan later on. This may provide additional flexibility until you decide where you ultimately want to invest the proceeds.

You will also be given the opportunity to cash out of your plan once you leave. This is a critical mistake. We understand that if you leave your job and don't have a new job lined up, it is very tempting to just take the check.

There are many disadvantages to choosing this option. You will have to pay taxes on the full amount that you receive and will most likely have some of the taxes withheld before you even receive your check. If you are under age 59 and a half, you will also have to pay a 10 percent penalty for taking the money before retirement. The biggest disadvantage of all is that you will have destroyed all of what you have been working for in this regard. By cashing out of the plan, you will be taking money today that you had earmarked for tomorrow. Do your best to avoid this choice, even though you may be very tempted to do so.

RETIREMENT MYTH #10

"Withdrawing money from my account when I leave this company won't really matter in the long run."

Think twice about this expensive mistake. Why give up to 40 percent or more of your account to taxes and penalties? This can all be avoided by rolling over your balance to your next employer's 401(k) plan or into a personal IRA rollover account.

Factors to be considered whether to roll your 401(k) account into your new employer's plan or an IRA include investment choice. You will be limited to the investment menu that your new company offers, but it may have everything you need to make good investment choices. An IRA allows for total flexibility because you can select from many different kinds of investments.

Another factor is cost. You must compare the costs of your

existing plan, the new company's 401(k) plan, and the expenses of the IRA you are considering. All of these fees can vary greatly, so be sure to include this consideration in your decision-making. If you're not sure of the costs, go back to Chapter Eight and review the three types of costs associated with investing.

Another thing to consider is that you may want to have the convenience of consolidating all of your accounts together, so it will be easier to keep track of. If your account balance is below $5,000 when you leave your job, be sure to roll your account to your new job's plan or an IRA as soon as possible, because your former employer can force you out of the plan and into an IRA account that they designate. This is usually for their convenience, not yours. The expenses of these accounts are usually high, and the investment choice is usually limited.

If your account is worth less than $1,000, they can send you a check, even though that isn't what you want done, and it subjects you to taxes and perhaps penalties. Therefore, do not put off the important decision of what to do for very long. You may be stuck with an unwanted outcome.

When you leave your job, make sure that you have no outstanding loans from your 401(k) account. If you do, pay them off as soon as possible after your last day of employment there. You have until the due date of your tax return (including extensions) to repay any loans you have taken from the plan, or you will default on the loan. That's because your method of paying back the loan—your paycheck—stops when you stop your employment.

If you default on the loan, you can expect your former plan to notify the Internal Revenue Service via an IRS Form 1099-R, which will report the unpaid amount. That amount will be treated as taxable income subject to income tax. If you're under age 59 and a half, you'll have to pay a 10 percent early withdrawal penalty, as well.

If you are leaving your company due to retirement, you also have choices about what to do with the money in your 401(k) account. You can keep it there and take money out as needed. You can roll the amount over into a rollover IRA account and be completely responsible for managing the account. Some plans allow you to take your money out in the form of an *annuity*, a guaranteed monthly benefit for the rest of your life.

The decision of how to invest your 401(k) account after you retire is a highly personal decision and should be made with the assistance of a professional advisor.

INVEST WITH ACCOUNTABILITY

⊘ When you change jobs, consider where to put your retirement account.

⊘ Don't cash out of the plan, if at all possible.

⊘ If retiring, plan your next course of action.

⊘ Be accountable to yourself.

FINAL THOUGHTS: COMMON FINANCIAL SENSE

"Do or do not. There is no try."

Retirement plans aren't for spectators. That's why those who invest in them are called *participants*. You are the sum of all the decisions you have made or decisions you have allowed others to make for you. Remember that all financial decisions have consequences. The consequences of the decisions you're making right now about committing to your financial future are about as big as they get. Take control and invest with common financial sense.

Take a moment to think about everything you've spent

money on in the last year. HYPFTIR? That's right—**H**ow **Y**ou **P**aying **F**or **T**hat **I**n **R**etirement? Consider this book as a visit by your future self, like the premise of the movie *Back to the Future*,[25] trying to gently guide you in the right direction.

It has been said that there are only three kinds of people: the ones who make things happen, the ones who watch things happen, and the ones who wonder what happened. You are ready to do this. It's planning, investing, and then monitoring your plan and investments.

Here's the equation: Amount invested into a diversified portfolio + Time + Patience = Highest chance of successfully attaining your retirement savings goal.

Risk matters. Limiting your losses is a key to wealth accumulation. This is not accomplished by trying to time the markets; that simply doesn't work. It is the consistency of returns that builds greater wealth over time and reduces the number of sleepless nights.

How you invest matters. There are no perfect investments. There are many considerations and trade-offs to make along the way.

Expenses matter. Fees and commissions that you save

---

25 *Back to the Future*, directed by Robert Zemeckis. Universal Pictures, 1985. Film.

over time can compound into significant wealth for you. Taxes matter, as well. The more tax-efficient you are, the less lost opportunity cost you have on income taxes that must be paid.

What matters most of all? Common financial sense. Knowing what you want matters. You need to know what you are saving and investing your money for. It may be a long time until retirement, but hopefully, you will spend a lot of years enjoying your retirement.

Remember these common financial sense ideas to help you on your journey toward a successful retirement. Identify how much money you'll need to retire. Get started now and know that saving a lot is great, saving some is good, but even saving a little is better than saving nothing at all.

Always be mindful of what you can control versus what you can't. Don't waste your energy worrying about things that you have no control over.

Know the three types of costs associated with retirement plans: overt, covert, and opportunity costs.

Understand that there are only nine kinds of stock investments you can make, and that there are three general types of retirement plan investments available to you: active, passive (index), and managed portfolios.

The most likely path for you depends on how much knowledge you have about the choices available in your plan, how much free time you have to monitor them, and how much inclination you have to spend your free time learning about this subject. Use time and compound interest to your advantage. Diversify and rebalance your account. Monitor your progress over time.

We hope that these ideas make common financial sense to you and will allow you to get a better handle on your financial future. We also hope that these strategies will help you to make good decisions that will lead to saving successfully for your retirement.

We'd like to hear from you about your progress. Please tell us your story at cfs@cfsias.com, and we will try to include it in our next book.

ABOUT THE AUTHORS

HARRIS NYDICK CFP®, AIFA®

HARRIS NYDICK is a cofounder of CFS Investment Advisory Services, L.L.C. A graduate of Syracuse University, he currently serves on the Investment Committee of the American Liver Foundation and is the vice president of the Jewish Community Foundation of Greater MetroWest New Jersey. He's been recognized by *Barron's*, *Financial Times*, and *Forbes* Best-In-State as one of the top wealth advisors in the country, and he frequently speaks and writes on the topic of retirement and financial planning.

GREG MAKOWSKI CFP®, AIF®

GREG MAKOWSKI is a graduate of William Paterson University and is a cofounder of CFS Investment Advisory Services, L.L.C. Greg currently serves on William Paterson University's Costakos College of Business Advisory and Advancement Board. He is a *Barron's* and *Forbes* Best-In-State top wealth advisor as well as a Five Star Wealth Manager. He has spoken at national industry conferences and has been featured in numerous publications and radio shows.

TED BENNA

TED BENNA is commonly referred to as the "father of 401(k)" because he created and gained IRS approval of the first 401(k) savings plan. He is a nationally recognized expert on retirement issues whose articles and comments have appeared in many publications.

Ted has received many citations for his accomplishments, including 2001 National Jefferson Award recipient for Greatest Public Service by a Private Citizen, 2001 Player of the Year selected by Defined Contribution News, one of eight individuals selected by *Money* magazine for its special 20th Anniversary Issue Hall of Fame, selected by *Business Insurance* as one the four People of the Century, one of ten selected by *Mutual Fund Market News* for its special 10th Anniversary Issue Legends in Our Own Time and 2005 Lifetime Achievement Award by Defined Contribution News. Ted has authored four books, the latest of which is *401(k) for Dummies*.

INDEX

costs
    basic, 70-71, 140, 143
    covert, 90-91, 155
    of healthcare, 47-50
    of inflation, *see* inflation
    of investing, 75-76, 88-92, 149-150, 154-155
    of retirement, 19, 42, 61-64
    of waiting 135-136
    per share, 100, 112
    see also, fees
counterintuitive markets, 111-112
credit, 139-141

D

debt, 71, 108, 113, 140-141
defined benefit pension plans, 18-20
defined contribution plans, 19
disability insurance, 141
discipline, 66, 69, 74, 84, 92, 97-98, 110, 112, 142
diversified portfolios, 113, 117, 140, 154, 156
dividend withdrawals, 145
"Dollar a Week" game, 72-73
dollar cost averaging, 97-100, 103
Dow Jones Industrial Average, 131

E

EBRI, 43
emergency funds, 140
emotions
    control of, 57, 81, 92
    energy and, 55
    health and, 39, 94
    in investing, 75-76, 81-84, 87, 92, 112
    versus logic, 27-28
Employee Benefit Research Institute, *see* EBRI
Employee Retirement Income Security Act, *see* ERISA
employer match, 88, 125-130
employment, length of, 88
employment changes, 147-152
ERISA, 19-20
estate plans, 146
excuses versus reasons, 69-70
expense ratio, 90
expenses, *see* costs

K

L

M

S

W

willpower, 58, 98
wills, 142, 146
withdrawal, 123, 145, 151
workers, older, 35-37
worry, 92-94, 118, 155

Y

yearly spending, 62-63
YOLO (You Only Live Once), 74

74257583R00105

Made in the USA
San Bernardino, CA
14 April 2018